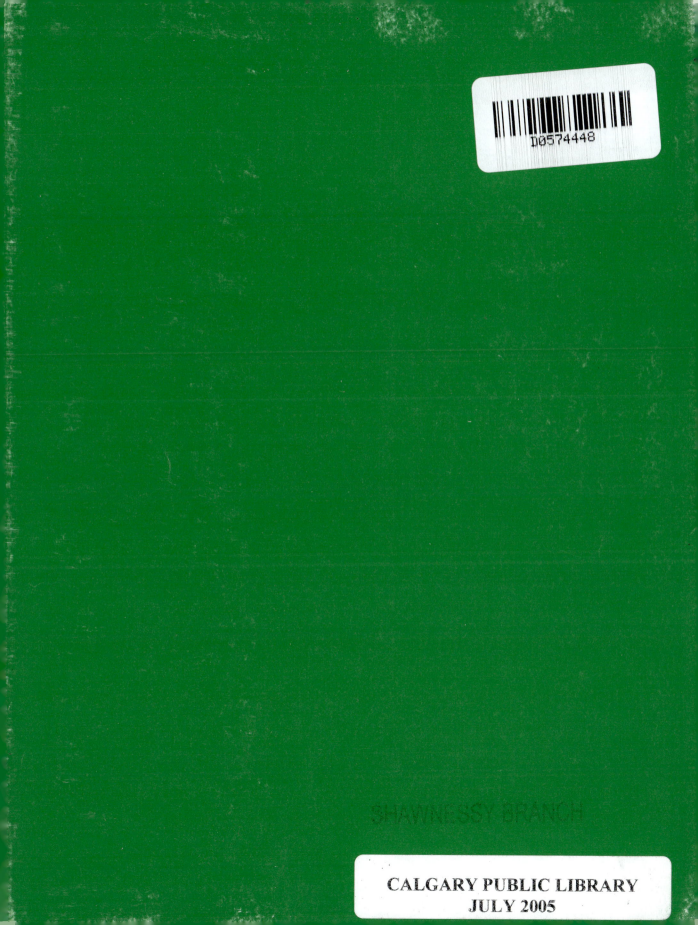

BUSHCRAFT
SURVIVAL

Also by Ray Mears

BUSHCRAFT

ESSENTIAL BUSHCRAFT

THE REAL HEROES OF TELEMARK

Ray Mears

BUSHCRAFT SURVIVAL

HODDER &
STOUGHTON

First published in Great Britain in 2005 by Hodder and Stoughton
A division of Hodder Headline

The right of Ray Mears to be identified as the Author of the Work has been
asserted by him in accordance with the Copyright, Designs and Patents Act
1988.

A Hodder and Stoughton book

1 3 5 7 9 10 8 6 4 2

By arrangement with the BBC
The BBC logo is a registered trademark of the British Broadcasting
Corporation and is used under licence
BBC logo © BBC 1996

A CIP catalogue record for this title is available from the British Library

ISBN 0 340 83480 3

Typeset in Adobe Garamond
Designed by Ned Hoste/2h
Printed and bound in Great Britain by Butler and Tanner

Hodder Headline's policy is to use papers that are natural, renewable and
recyclable products and made from wood grown in sustainable forests. The
logging and manufacturing processes are expected to conform to the
environmental regulations of the country of origin.

Hodder and Stoughton Ltd
A division of Hodder Headline
338 Euston Road
London NW1 3BH

Contents

Aboriginal Britain

6,000 years ago a forest of oak, yew and hazel
grew here on the banks of the River Thames
in London. To see these primeval tree stumps
and then look up at the modern buildings
around is an extraordinary glimpse of our past
– and our future.

For more than half a million years Britons lived as nomadic hunter-gatherers, but we know very little about our aboriginal ancestors because they left behind only the scantiest traces of their existence. Most of the artefacts of our Stone Age culture have long since been reclaimed by the earth. Looking at our prehistory is like peering through a keyhole, but when we do get an insight into that ancient world, it is utterly fascinating.

Such a glimpse into the past can be experienced from the banks of the Thames Estuary where 6,000-year-old tree stumps, the remnants of a Stone Age forest, emerge from the mudflats at low tide every day, just a few miles upstream from the towering office blocks of the City of London. To look at one, and then the other, is to see history come alive and we can not help but feel a thrilling connection with our past; a powerful sense of how radically the British landscape and the life of its inhabitants have changed in just a few centuries. Where once we stalked wild animals in dense woodland and fished along the riverbanks, we now emerge from underground trains and disappear into the labyrinths of great buildings in search of a different kind of livelihood.

If we look closely at the tree stumps in the Thames, we can even identify the species of yew, oak and hazel – trees which still adorn the British countryside today – and it takes only a small step of the imagination to form a picture of how our land must have looked all those centuries ago. Those who have seen the stumps probably imagine them to have lain there for no more than a few decades, unaware that in fact they were standing before Stonehenge was built. The people who lived and hunted among them were thoroughly modern humans, the final generations of a hunter-gatherer culture with highly sophisticated bushcraft skills. What I find remarkable is that some of the skills practised by our nomadic forebears were still being put to use on the Thames, and elsewhere, just a few generations ago. We know that people were still fishing for flounder on the Thames using hawthorns as hooks at the turn of the twentieth century, just as Stone Age man had done on exactly the same stretch of waterway all those millennia ago.

I recreated my own fishing line by tying up a series of baited hawthorns and laying it out over the mudflats. The technique of using loops rather than knots to fasten the hooks to the line is astonishingly simple and effective and when I returned at the next low tide twelve hours later, it was a thrilling moment to find three flounder flapping in their muddy pools. I experienced another tangible link with our distant past when I picked up a hazelnut, which I planned to give to a botanist friend, only for it to disintegrate into dust in my hand. In that one instance I felt an electrifying connection with our primeval ancestors.

We are told today that the Thames is cleaner than it has been for centuries, and that the return of salmon is proof of its regeneration. That is to be welcomed as progress, but we are still not asking the questions that the hunter-gatherer would have asked, namely: 'Are the salmon spawning? Is there going to be a good salmon run here next year? Should I come back here with my family to fish, or shall I try another location?' Perhaps we should be asking ourselves those questions our

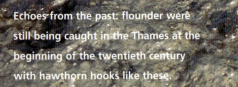

Echoes from the past: flounder were
still being caught in the Thames at the
beginning of the twentieth century
with hawthorn hooks like these.

With Britain covered by dense forest during the Stone Age, seas, lakes and rivers were very important routes for travel and trade.

species was posing itself 5,000 or so years ago, to guide us today and inspire us to be more demanding of our authorities, and to enshrine laws that make it possible for us to look after our countryside in a way that will mimic as closely as possible the pristine environment that our ancestors once enjoyed.

The Stone Age era makes up roughly 98 per cent of the time-span that mankind has roamed the planet and yet we know virtually nothing about the origins of our culture. As nomads living in caves or makeshift tents, they left behind no monuments or permanent structures. There were no lasting settlements because people moved on to new locations, according to the seasons, in anticipation of the natural bounty to be found there. Our ancestors had to be entirely in tune with their natural surroundings, and their decisions to move on were determined by an instinctive knowledge, based on thousands of years of experience. Their calendar was written in the behaviour of the wildlife around them. The flowering of a certain plant, for instance, or the arrival of geese, were important calendar events that determined their movements.

The archaeological evidence of Stone Age culture is limited mainly to flint and stone tools, as well as some animal bones and antlers, which were put to various practical and religious purposes, and also a few examples of cave art. There are no faces or voices to help us interpret our ancient way of life, just a few fragments in the dirt. Today we are literally picking up the pieces of what they left behind in order to understand what kind of world they lived in and how they not only survived, but thrived in it. It is perhaps the most incredible feature of our hunter-gathering ancestors that they left virtually no impact on the world in which they lived – just the odd heap of ashes and stones from a fire, a pile of discarded shellfish on a shoreline, or the occasional figure of an animal daubed onto a cave wall.

What we do know about our prehistory is that for thousands of years we were all hunter-gatherers, roaming Britain's dense forests and bountifully stocked shorelines for our means of living. Around 8000–7000 BC the first farming settlements started to emerge in the Middle East but in Britain we did not become an agricultural people for three or four thousand years after that. In the relatively short period since then, a vast knowledge of bushcraft, accumulated over tens of thousands of millennia by our Stone Age ancestors, began to disappear rapidly.

One other fact of which we can be certain is that our ancestors generally lived very well, enjoying the pickings of a land rich in natural produce as they trod a well-worn circuit around the country in step with the shifting seasons. In Britain's vast ancient woodlands they hunted big game such as wild cattle, deer and boar; they trapped smaller animals; they fished on coasts, lakes and rivers; and they gathered wild berries and other fruits, vegetables, seeds and nuts. In order to survive, our ancestors needed to have a profound knowledge of their habitat. They had to understand the migration patterns of the deer herds, as well as where and at what time of year particular fruits and vegetables, fish and shellfish were available in quantities large enough to sustain a travelling community.

Surviving examples of British bushcraft are rare and one of the reasons for this is that our landscape has changed beyond all recognition in just a few centuries. Where now there are agricultural fields, urban communities, roads and industrial installations, there once stood endless expanses of dense, deciduous forest. It is no exaggeration to say that if you had walked from one end of Britain to the other you would have barely been able to see the land for the trees. The canopy spread over our island was like a giant deciduous jungle, broken only by river courses and the occasional stretch of heathland and rocky outcrop. Although most of the species of trees would be recognisable to us, we would have been taken aback by their size. The lie of the land, however, has changed little since the last Ice Age and, as I pant my way up one of Britain's hills or mountains, I find it exhilarating to know that my aboriginal ancestor would have been doing exactly the same all those years ago.

It is estimated that the population of Britain around 7500 BC during the Mesolithic era (the Middle Stone Age) would have been no more than about ten thousand – all living in small family-based bands and sharing the spoils of the woods with wolves and bears. One of the joys of modern bushcraft is learning to see the landscape around you through the eyes of the indigenous locals, because it transforms the view and understanding of your natural surroundings. When I walk through what remains of our beautiful woodland today I try to imagine scenes from the past: the smell of venison being cooked over a camp fire drifting through the boughs, or the sound of a flint axe hacking at a branch to be used for shelter.

I also look at the plants which were of the greatest interest and importance to our Stone Age ancestors and were put to a wide variety of practical applications. Sphagnum moss, for instance, which is found in dense clusters in swamps, bogs and ponds, is a highly versatile, mildly antiseptic plant with a peculiar physical structure that allows it to hold up to twenty times its own weight in water. It was used variously by our aboriginal forefathers as a sponge, a sanitary towel, a wound dressing and a nappy, as well as bedding for both man and beast and as a form of natural 'bubble wrap' for carrying young children, or precious goods like flint axes.

Just as our natural surroundings today can help us to invoke a vision of our nomadic past, the smallest man-made artefacts discovered by archaeologists in modern times can give us a clear insight into what life must have been like. Stone, especially flint, was a precious material for our aboriginal ancestors in Britain and for well over 500,000 years it was coveted and traded for its use in the making of various tools, implements and weapons, including axes, blades, spears and harpoons, which were all essential items of equipment for survival in a hunter-gatherer culture.

The evolution of man in the Stone Age period is mirrored in the development of his flint-working techniques. A highly sophisticated stone-tool culture, what we would call 'flint-knapping' today, developed over those half a million years, but today there are only a small handful of people left on the planet who practise this ancient skill. For me John Lord is the best flint-knapper in the country and it has been through listening to his knowledge and observing his skills that I have been able to appreciate the tremendous technical expertise of our forebears. 'These people were incredible craftsmen,' says John. 'When you are working with stone today, you feel a direct link with the past.'

As populations grew and the demand for flint intensified, man was forced, quite literally, to go to greater depths to find it. Mining for the material and making tools from it became one of man's earliest commercial enterprises. Evidence of a remarkable Stone Age flint industry has been discovered at a mine called Grimes Graves near Thetford Forest in Norfolk. The mine, which dates back between 2,200 to 2,500 years, consisted of 350 shafts, some of them up to 30 feet deep, which is incredible when you consider that the Neolithic miners had only antlers and animal bones to dig through the chalky earth. Tools made from these mines have been found as far away as Scotland.

Most of the flint tools and other Stone Age artefacts to have been discovered in this country have found their way into the vaults of the British Museum. Dr Jill Cook, who works in the prehistory department of the museum, is a leading expert on Stone Age culture and for me she is the true

John Lord, flint-knapper: 'When you are working with stone today you feel a direct link with the past.'

Coastal, river and lakeside shorelines were important sources
of food for ancestors – and beachcombing is still fun today.

keeper of this country's crown jewels and our glorious heritage. She has a great passion for her subject and when I went to visit her at the British Museum I sat transfixed as she showed me the many Stone Age artefacts kept in her vaults. One tiny fish hook in particular, engraved with a picture of a fish taking the bait on a line, provided a wonderful insight, as good as any photograph, into our deep past.

Jill is in no doubt about the technical ingenuity of our aboriginal ancestors: 'They were a highly sophisticated people and by the end of the last Ice Age, circa 12,000 BC, people had developed very advanced bushcraft skills. They were not just eking out a living on the edge, but took full opportunity of the natural abundance around them. It is clear too that they had a spiritual and an artistic life, which we only get tiny glimpses of through the archaeology.'

Most of the tools and equipment used and carried by Stone Age man were made from natural materials such as animal skins and wood and they have long since disintegrated and perished in our acidic soil. One of the handful of objects to survive the great passage of time since the Stone Age is what has come to be known as the 'Ashcott Heath bow', named after the area of Somerset in which it was discovered over 4,700 years after it was lost or discarded by its owner. The weapon, made from yew, is a forerunner of the medieval longbow which was used to decisive advantage by English soldiers in the battles of Crécy, Poitiers and Agincourt in the Hundred Years' War with France. One of the extraordinary features of the Ashcott Heath bow is that its makers chose a less than ideal piece of wood from which to create it. Chris Boyton, the country's top bow-maker today, explains: 'Normally in wooden bow-making, the back face of the bow is made out of the outer part of the yew tree, using a thin white band of sapwood which is very elastic. But in this instance they have removed that and used the solid, less flexible heart of the tree. Any knots and defects can wreck a bow because a bow needs to flex equally in all places – if one area is weak or stiff, the load isn't evenly distributed and that will generally lead to it snapping. But despite the poor quality of the material the workmanship on it is still very, very good when you consider that they were using stone tools.'

The invention of the bow caused a
revolution in hunting technology.

1, 2 and 3: I'm familiar with using an adze but it was a totally new experience for Chris. With his innate craftsmanship to the fore it wasn't long before he was using it to great effect to shape the bow stave. 4: Arrow-making with a flint tool. 5: Trying out the finished bow.

Leaving our modern tools and workshop behind, Chris and I attempted to make a Stone Age longbow using Stone Age materials and techniques. Using my knowledge of flint tools and bushcraft, and Chris's bow-making skills, we based our design exactly on the Ashcott Heath model. My task was to make the arrows and for that I had to make a fire the Stone Age way by striking flints against iron pyrites for a spark to ignite the horse hoof fungus used as tinder. The sparks from pyrites are not that hot so the tinder has to be very well prepared by scraping it into a large bunch of cotton wool-style fibre; when a spark eventually takes hold in the tinder you blow on it gently, until you have a good enough flame to add some kindling to it.

Yew is a very good wood for making a bow because it has excellent spring and has tremendous strength and flexibility. It is, however, a 'thoroughbred wood' and not easy to work with, demanding the highest craft skills to fashion it into an effective weapon. Most Stone Age arrows that have been found are made from viburnum shoots, which are naturally straight and have a tremendous stiffness capable of withstanding the heavy draw of the bow, but there was no viburnum to hand on our site, so I opted to use hazel branches instead. As the branches were fairly green I dried them out over the heat of a fire before straightening them out by hand and then scraping and sanding them into the finished article. Accuracy was essential for ancient hunters and to achieve it they needed the shaft of the arrow to be as straight as possible because even minor kinks and knots can cause the arrow to wobble in flight.

The woods in which we worked would have been the equivalent of the DIY store and the supermarket for Stone Age man and to underline the point I made Chris and myself a Stone Age snack to keep us going. All around us lay the roots of the celandine plant – which are very easy to collect – and I simply baked them in a scrape under the fire for a few minutes. The roots, which have a lovely sweet-potato taste, are full of starch and are ideal for the supply of energy – as simple and delicious as a bowl of chips.

You need some kind of glue to affix the arrowheads to the shaft and for that I used dry pine resin which I chipped from the bark of a tree and then placed next to the fire in order to melt it. The resin is as brittle as glass when it dries, so charcoal is added to help strengthen it. Our ancestors would have used a number of different fibres to tie on the arrowhead, and on this occasion we used the long strings from the stalks of the stinging nettle which are very durable. Finally we attached the feather fletching to the base of the shaft using the leg tendons from a red deer that we had pounded into fine fibres, which are strong and also contain their own natural glue. Finally, just as our Stone Age ancestors would have done, I chewed up some bluebell bulbs for glue, but took care not to swallow the pulp which is very poisonous.

Today it is illegal to bow-hunt in Britain, but we can still explore with the eyes of a hunter, just as our Stone Age ancestors did. The edge of a forest near a lake, pond or river would have given them the ability to prey on woodland animals coming to drink. Away from the protection of the trees, the animals were exposed and vulnerable to ambush from the bank, or from dugout canoes on the water. The remains of butchered wild horse and boar as well as great crested grebe and teal ducks have all been found by archaeologists on Britain's banks and shores, but there was one animal above all that Stone Age man coveted and pursued: the deer.

Aboriginal Britons, who followed the deer herds as they migrated around the country, were expert trackers familiar with every detail of their prey's behaviour, like nomadic people in other parts of the world today. One of the most profound aspects of living tribal cultures I have experienced is their respect for the animals that they hunt. Their prey are treated with reverence, as if they were brothers or cousins in the natural world, all sharing and living off the same surroundings. Many cultures believe that if you do not treat animals with respect you will have no luck as a hunter. The ancient Britons were no exception and they had a powerful spiritual relationship with the natural world around them.

At Starr Carr in East Yorkshire, archaeologists have discovered a campsite used by hunters living at the end of the Stone Age. Animal bones from the site show that the hunters killed a range of large game animals including deer, wild cattle, moose and wild pigs. The site is particularly important because it sheds light on how our Mesolithic ancestors were dictated to by the change of seasons. Amongst the artefacts they have discovered is a set of what are believed to be head-dresses, about twenty of them, which were made from the craniums and antlers of red deer. We cannot be entirely certain about the use of these head-dresses, but one possibility is that they were worn as camouflage for stalking deer, allowing hunters to mimic the behaviour of their prey and to get up close to them before firing their

Butchering a roe deer with my versions of Stone Age implements proves how good our forebears were at tool-making.

arrows. Another possibility is that the hunters used them as some sort of mask for religious purposes, perhaps trying to imbue themselves with the power and prowess of the beasts they spent a lifetime hunting. The belief that the essence of an animal can be captured by wearing a mask it resembles can still be found in many native societies today.

For our ancestors the carcass of a deer was a precious prize. The antlers and bones were an incredibly important resource from which they could make needles, harpoon points and tools; the juice of the eyeball could be used as a glue and the skin for bedding, clothing, bags and ropes. The deer tendon is very tough material which, when dried, pounded and torn into thin strips, could be used for all manner of purposes, such as sewing and binding materials.

As our aboriginal ancestors did not have any forms of pot or pan at their disposal, they had to use other means to cook their meat. They did this by burning a fire into the ground and lining it with flat rocks which absorb the heat very well. Once the rocks were hot enough the hunters would have removed them to form a makeshift oven, placing the meat between them

From this roe deer carcass we get food, bone, sinew and skin – a rich harvest for our Stone Age ancestors.

before sealing the oven with a lid made up of sticks and moss, finished with sand or earth to make it airtight. The hunters would have used this same simple technique to cook one small joint of meat or to prepare a feast for dozens. Cooked in this fashion, the meat is as good as any I have ever tasted.

If his migration pattern led him to the shores and estuaries, Stone Age man would have enjoyed a feast of delicious seafood during his stay. Alaskan Indians have a saying: 'When the tide is out, the table is set.' That is how it must have been for our ancestors too and it is no wonder that they clung to Britain's shorelines as the abundance and diversity of foods available was tremendous: limpets, razor clams, cockles, mussels – which could all be

Three essential resources of Stone Age Britain:
wood, fire and antler.

cooked and eaten within minutes of being gathered, simply by covering
them with hot ashes. I do not know why we do not eat more razor clams in
Britain these days because they are simply delicious. The gastronomes of
France, however, do share the Stone Age love of these delicacies and you can
find them in top restaurants in Paris today.

We know that Stone Age Britons cooked seafood in this way for
millennium after millennium because archaeologists have discovered piles of
their shells dotted around the country's shores. Highlighting the richness
and diversity of the aboriginal diet, the bones of deer, wild boar and seals
have also been found in the great mounds of refuse that were formed over
the years as generations of nomadic communities returned to the same site.

Bushcraft never wastes a resource and, just as my Stone Age ancestors
would have done, I packed up my horse hoof fungus tinder, which can
smoulder for up to twelve hours, and kept it for use the following day. If
you were living a nomadic lifestyle, this prehistoric 'lighter' was a superb
device for saving both time and labour as you could carry it with you on a
day's trek. At the next location you could enjoy the benefits of a good fire
within minutes of arrival simply by adding some dry kindling to the tinder.

Hunting and gathering demands a highly practical and resourceful approach to daily life, but recent discoveries have shown that our distant ancestors enjoyed a spiritual and artistic life as well. We know from archaeological evidence that our ancestors made very good use of rocky outcrops and caves, which were ideal for shelter from the elements and wild animals, and it is in these places that some of the earliest forms of human artwork can be found. Spectacular examples of aboriginal art, dating back 17,000 years, have been uncovered in continental Europe, mainly in France and Spain, but it was not until 2003 that the first cave image was discovered in Britain. A year later archaeologists announced the discovery of the most remarkable examples of prehistoric cave art within our shores.

Described as the Sistine Chapel of the Ice Age, the artwork at Creswell Crags in Nottinghamshire is thought to be about 13,000 years old and includes sophisticated images of deer, bear, bison and several species of birds. The detail and accuracy of the animal anatomies depicted in much European cave art reveals a high degree of technical skill. These are no mere scribblings on a wall – as I discovered myself when I tried my hand at some cave artwork using Stone Age materials and techniques. Pigment, such as red ochre, was used either as a kind of crayon or it was ground up and mixed with water or spit to form a paste. For the finer details, brushes were made with animal hairs tied onto the end of a stick, just as they are today, and to fill in the larger areas they used animal skin wrapped around wet sphagnum moss and tied it up with a strip of leather to form a sponge.

When you consider that they had only the dim light of a fire in which to work, the achievements of prehistoric cave artists become all the more remarkable and for me, they provide conclusive proof, if it was needed, that the culture of our aboriginal ancestors was far more advanced than previously imagined.

The Yekuana
river people of the Amazon

*No matter how many times
I return to the jungle
I always forget just how
awe-inspiring it is.*

Although the television series started with an archaeological retrospective of our aboriginal past, the filming began a long way from the Mesolithic forest of Britain in a steamy South American rainforest. I have always loved forests. It was tracking wildlife through the woods of the North Downs as a boy that sparked and then fuelled my fascination with bushcraft. I can still clearly remember the sense of joy and freedom that came from padding silently down those gloomy tracks under the oaken canopy, equipped with only an old biscuit tin to cook in and an old army poncho. Even today my enthusiasm for British woodland is undiminished, I feel a spring in my step and my senses relax into the alertness required to appreciate the wildlife of my native woodland. Without realising it, those days spent exploring the woods of Surrey and Sussex were perfect preparation for journeys into other forests – some so large that they seem to be living entities in their own right.

Forests come in many forms, but the busiest and most challenging to come to grips with are tropical rainforests. In many ways jungle is the ultimate forest, and what you find in the Amazonian basin is the ultimate jungle. The sheer scale, density and diversity of the rainforest is staggering. There are places where no human has ever set foot – and hopefully never will. In a world shrunk by air travel and increasingly sophisticated technology, the remoteness of the jungle is awe-inspiring, and the abundance of its natural riches confounds the imagination. To enter this vast jungle of northern South America is to step back in time, to experience an ancient natural world almost entirely cut off from the outside.

Some of the main enticements jungles hold for the forest traveller are their great secrets, from lost cities to species yet to be recorded by scientists. But it would be wrong to envisage a forest devoid of people. The Amazon basin is in many ways like a great housing estate. Beneath the forest canopy villages are connected by a network of foot trails and rivers which follow ancient trading routes and a mosaic of tribal territories.

We had arranged to visit a village called Kanarakuni to live among the Yekuana, an ancient river people from the Venezuelan area of the forest in the Guiana Highlands, close to the Brazilian border. The ease of modern travel creates a false sense of accessibility. One day we were checking in our

luggage in London, the next we were preparing to fly out of Ciudad Bolivar in an ageing Antonov. With the pilot hurrying us so that he would have sufficient daylight to make a return flight, a local fixer handed us a last meal of Big Macs and fries. I ate reluctantly: I hadn't expected to find a McDonald's here, on the border of what is mostly an uncharted forest territory the size of Australia. It didn't seem to bode well. McDonald's was not here when I last passed through Ciudad Bolivar; as we ate it seemed, perhaps unfairly, to symbolise the incredible pace at which the world is currently changing. Whenever I have encountered the modern world reaching out to wild corners of our planet the result is environmental disaster – and a tragic demise of complex, but unvalued, human cultures. With the journey pressing we were thankful for the nourishment and happy that despite reaching the edge of the vast wilderness of the rainforest and its ancient tribes, McDonald's had reached the frontier, and for the time being could go no further.

We could have travelled to Kanarakuni by boat, but it would have taken us weeks to get there because the long, winding river route is punctuated by waterfalls and rapids. The people of this area keep dugout canoes both above and below the falls to avoid having to carry them up and down the great precipices over which the waters cascade. These falls are a major natural obstruction in the region that effectively bar expansion and penetration, helping to preserve the local cultures from unwanted outside influences, while at the same moment having the negative effect of reducing access to modern healthcare.

The sheer enormity of this forest is beyond the perception of human imagination. Even from a plane you can see only a tiny part of its two and a half million square miles. You have to look at a map to understand how big it is in relation to the rest of the earth. If you have sharp eyes you will occasionally see a little settlement as you fly over, but otherwise it is just hour after hour of trees and rivers that resemble an endless carpet of moss. All you can see is green, with no sense of the trees' great height, just a vast leafy expanse.

During our flight I turned on my Global Positioning System (GPS) to discover our exact location. I watched with fascination as the latitude and longitude figures ticked away, enabling me to plot our progress on a chart. After passing over a series of remote gold mines

The Amazon wilderness may be shrinking but parts of it still defy technology: some areas have not yet been mapped so a GPS (Global Positioning System) doesn't always help.

the chart showed that, like sixteenth-century mariners, we had passed into uncharted territory. The display read: 'Relief Data Incomplete'. Below us was an endless expanse of forest, broken only by the river Paragua and its tributaries. It reminded me of an earlier flight into the region when I had looked down and glimpsed a forest Indian in a canoe; he was looking up from a river in an area inhabited by a tribe that has barely any contact with the world beyond.

Flights into this rainforest are bizarre. As the small aircraft threads its way between stacks of cumulus cloud the journey seems tedious, yet at the same moment you know that it is a snip compared to traversing the landscape below on foot. Plush airliners give way to the peeling cream paint and tarnished aluminium air frames of rickety light aircraft as you are transported to a land that time seems to have forsaken. As the plane descended we could see the canopy buzzing with life, as parrots, macaws and monkeys swooped from tree to tree. A clearing appeared on a bend in the river – a dozen or so buildings on a mere pinprick of open ground. Before we had time to take it all in, our little plane was bouncing awkwardly along the uneven grass airstrip.

As the aircraft taxied towards the village at the end of the grass strip I could already see most of the villagers standing watching with the fascination that I have witnessed so many times before and yet which is impossible to fathom from our perspective. Around 120 people live in Kanarakuni and most of them had turned out to greet us. One particular piece of our cargo was carried carefully to the huts. This was the outboard

Kanarakuni: traditionally, all the families would have lived
together in one large hut like the one on the left.

motor we had promised them as part of their 'fee' for allowing us to film their way of life. I felt wary about this: I have immense respect for ancient cultures and indigenous people, so while the engine would improve the lives of the people in the area, it also meant they would have less use for their traditional paddles. The motor would help them to improve their lives but might contribute to the undermining of their *way* of life. They were very happy with it, though, and my discomfort was tempered by the realisation that the erosion of traditional customs is an inevitable process that has been taking place ever since the Amazon was opened up by Christian missionaries. You cannot reverse the process. If they hadn't obtained the engine from us, they would have traded for it from somewhere else, at a cost that can only be guessed. At least we were trading it for the knowledge of traditional skills.

Life in Kanarakuni is a mixture of change and tradition. While the Yekuana are still masters of their own culture and destiny, they willingly supplement their traditional lifestyle with a handful of goods from outside. Everywhere in the village there are bizarre reminders of the world beyond

The designs woven into the baskets all tell a story: each motif has a particular significance.

the forest. T-shirts advertise western products, a testament to the steady encroachment of outside commercialism and the threat it poses to their independence. They are alert to the possible consequences of this encroachment but uncertain how to deal with it.

Traditionally Yekuana communities would live together in one communal thatched roundhouse with wattle and daub walls, partitioned inside for each individual family. Today though each family has its own group of similar but much smaller huts. The large central hut still survives, used for important village meetings, political rallies, parties and discos. Our first night at Kanarakuni was spent in a house set aside for visitors, providing us the necessary time for formal greetings, to arrange our logistics and simply to come to know some of the people with whom we would be working. This time is always essential and provides the necessary footing for a successful relationship with the community. I have been fortunate that the majority of the production teams I have worked with share my belief that filming in remote communities is a two-way process. Consequently we endeavour to make the experience something that all those involved will look back on with enjoyment. Friendships are not bought with gifts and trinkets but earned through discussion, frankness and by taking a genuine interest.

The next day we set off down the river in search of a suitable place to pitch camp. My intent was to base ourselves sufficiently far away from the village so that our Yekuana guides would have to rely upon their bushcraft. Close to the village the temptation would be to take the easy route, like someone camping in their back garden. Also, the natural resources around a village are nearly always exhausted, compared to an area of pristine forest. As we passed downriver by canoe we came across a sobering reminder of what can happen when things go wrong for visitors – the wreckage of a DC-3, which had crashed forty years earlier after the pilot and his crew had overshot the runway at Kanarakuni. Apparently they had been drinking, but, amazingly, they all survived.

Whenever an expedition ventures out into remote country the individual members of the party must be skilled in self-reliance, capable of dealing with all manner of emergencies and problems. Three villagers were chosen by the village chief to accompany us – Luís, Saul and Benito. For them, bushcraft is a way of

This propeller from a crashed plane is a grim reminder that although technology has made these remote areas more accessible, you should never take this terrain for granted.

life. I struck up a particularly good rapport with Luís, the oldest of the three and a highly respected figure in the Yekuana community. He is a walking encyclopaedia on the traditions and folklore of the forest. One of the things that has always struck me about the people who live in this forest is the strength with which they relate to the traditions of their life. Some are 'forest Indians', others 'Indians of the forest edge'. The Yekuana are 'river Indians' so before we set out, Benito demonstrated how to make a paddle with his machete. As he told me, 'If you don't know where your paddle is, you are not a Yekuana.' As I watched him at work, I reflected that Yekuana technology is no less sophisticated than our own – it's just different.

We found a clearing by the river that was perfect for a camp as it had been swept clear of vegetation by earlier floods. With little leaf matter about, we were less likely to encounter potentially dangerous insects or reptiles. And, with the major rains passed, the river was unlikely to burst its banks. The site's other advantage was that nature would clear away our fireplaces and any structures we built when the high waters returned. I have always believed that a basic principle of modern bushcraft is to minimise our impact on the forest environment and pass without leaving a trace.

I like to travel light. Bushcraft teaches you how to improvise, or to do without the clutter of everyday life: instead you learn to rely upon your understanding and knowledge of the natural world. The jungle is not always an easy place to travel in, and good bushcraft makes all the difference when you're there.

I planned to set up a fairly elaborate lightweight camp because we were going to be there for some time. The first thing to do in the rainforest environment is to put up a lightweight tarp roof. If it is pouring with rain you can keep dry as you work underneath – it's difficult to think straight with rain pounding on your head and

Wasps have an important role in the eco-system of the jungle – and some species can inflict a painful sting.

Manioc is an important source of carbohydrate and a staple food in this part of the world. Pounded into a pulp to remove certain toxic elements, it is then made into flour and used to make a kind of flat bread. Once heated over the fire, the bread is dried outdoors (overleaf).

Manioc bread drying in the sun. Notice the dog taking advantage of the shade cast by the giant circular bread!

On the left of the picture on page 49 is Luís, one of the most
respected of the Yekuana elders: keeper of knowledge and skills, it
is a privilege to travel with people like him.

accidents are more likely to happen. Even if the weather seems fine, a huge downpour is never far away. With the heat and humidity of the jungle sapping your energy, it is lovely to climb into a hammock beneath a tarp at the end of the day and listen to the rain hammering down all around, while you are comfy and dry. There is surely no better way to fall asleep – a hammock allows you to be both inside and outside. It's safe yet open to the freshness and vital energy of the jungle. It raises you up off the ground away from the splash zone of the rain, away from poisonous reptiles, spiders and above all the tiny, biting ants. Although we like to generalise, every rainforest is subtly different from its neighbour. Having been lucky enough to travel in more types of rainforest than most, I am alert to the differences. In some it is fine to sleep on the forest floor but here in the Amazonian forests the insects make this the land of the hammock. Every group of Indians I have travelled with here use hammocks and can, when necessary, fashion one from natural materials. Every Yekuana boy is taught how to make a shelter from leaves, beneath which he can sling a hammock made quickly from strips of flexible bark. The smoke from a small fire will keep insects away, but there are other hazards: black widow spiders, whose venom is fifteen times more toxic than that of a rattlesnake, are commonly found here. I was answering a call of nature in the middle of the night and noticed one crawling into my trousers. I flicked it away – but it was a useful reminder to be on my guard.

The Yekuana often travel long distances, mainly for trade, and can be away from home for weeks, even months. To make a journey in this environment they must be able to move quickly

Pit latrine – note candle for night-time use.

because the distances involved are vast, and to live off the land because it is not possible to carry enough food for long periods. The rainforest is not a place for the bushcraft beginner to go on their own – even the Yekuana rarely travel alone, except for short distances.

With the fundamentals in place, you can think about 'luxuries'. A second tarp to create a living space and to protect the cooking fire; a pit latrine measuring four feet by two, should last four people for at least two weeks. The sandy earth dug out is used to cover over deposits, thereby reducing the unpleasant odours and preventing a swarm of flies near the camp. Leave a candle next to the pit so that during the night you can check that no snakes have fallen into it.

We needed a bench, too, so that we could sit comfortably off the ground around the fire in the evenings. There is no shortage of building materials in the rainforest, which is dense with small saplings struggling to reach light. Thousands are packed into any small area but as only a few make it to the top, plenty of stiff timbers of different heights and diameters are available. They are perfect for construction as they are very straight and strong. The vines that hang from them are as strong as wire and will bind together the wood poles, and you can even split them so they go further. They are evidence of the rainforest's incredible biology: most plants move towards the light from the moment they emerge, but at the start of their life these lianas search for a suitable tree to climb, then turn 90 degrees and race for the top of the canopy. One of the great joys of bushcraft comes from the direct way we utilise natural resources, bringing us into immediate contact with nature as we use the specialised adaptations of various plants.

One evening, while I was collecting wood, I saw what looked like a palm tree and took a chop at it with my machete – only to discover it was a piece of aluminium aircraft fuselage from the crashed DC-3 upstream. The blow took a small nick out of the blade. The machete is the most valuable tool in the forest – a local man told me a great story to illustrate this. Some Yekuana were travelling downriver in powerful rapids and their canoe was about to capsize. They had to make a snap decision: did they take their packs, with all the food and cooking equipment, or hold on to their machetes? Every man came to the same conclusion: with his machete and his knowledge of bushcraft he could live indefinitely in the forest and work his way home.

While the machete, or parang, is the number one tool for jungle travel it is also the most dangerous piece of equipment used in bushcraft because of the length of its sharp blade and the commitment with which it is swung. While local people learn to use these tools by growing up around them, outsiders are not born with an innate knowledge of the machete and need to be taught its safe and proper use.

The jungle is a beautiful but harsh environment, with all life there in competition. Average temperatures of 40 degrees centigrade and high humidity mean it is vital to drink frequently. Inevitably, during the day clothes remain soaked from either rain or perspiration. Almost as soon as we exert ourselves we become drenched in sweat. At the end of each day I like to go down to a river and wash, if possible also rinsing out the salt and grime from my clothing. For comfort we keep two sets of clothes. Wet clothes, which as the name suggests remain more or less permanently soaked, are for day wear and our sets of dry clothes are kept for the evening, religiously sealed in dry bags. One of the greatest joys of each day is relaxing in my hammock and massaging and powdering my feet to prevent foot rot. While in Venezuela I heard of tourists who were so paranoid about stepping on anything poisonous that they didn't take off their boots

The razor-sharp parang, or machete, is ideal for making feather sticks for firelighting. The parang is the essential tool for jungle living and the Yekuana are rarely found without theirs.

for a whole week even when they were sleeping. Such paranoia is misplaced and potentially debilitating: the rainforest is a beautiful environment that we should learn to relax in. For the Yekuana, who run naked as young children, clothes seem just a nicety. They told me that when clothes were first introduced to the Indians of the region they were not told of the importance of washing them and consequently developed sores and skin complaints which they had never known when walking as nature intended.

For convenience we had brought most of our food from England in the form of lightweight rations. In contrast the Yekuana eat whatever they find in the forest and the river, including fruit, fish and capybara – the world's largest rodent. Their staple food is manioc bread, made from the root of the cassava plants grown in clearings near the village. When they travel through the forest they will bring one of these breads broken into plate-sized pieces for ease of carrying. While out collecting medicinal plants they surprised me by making an impromptu sandwich with this bread and live earthworms. We all chuckled at this sight not so much for its strangeness but because it reminded us of a hamburger. But what a marvellous lesson in survival. Worms, though disgusting to refined western sensibility, are an easily gathered source of protein, and collecting them in this impromptu way is a beautifully direct solution to hunger. Generally, my experience of working with hunter-gatherer groups has taught me that they rely far more heavily on smaller food resources than we

There are all sorts of amazing fauna in jungle pools and rivers: these are two cane toads mating.

may imagine. For example, another key Yekuana food are the large frogs found along the river. They are hunted at night with homemade head lamps to locate and dazzle them. A dozen or so large frogs thrown into a pot of boiling water with some salt make a substantial evening meal for three or four.

It's always a great education to be around people like the Yekuana. The diversity of their diet is matched only by the range of methods they employ to secure their food. Despite our huge supermarkets our average diet is far less diverse – and, I suspect, far less healthy for that lack of variety.

One of my strongest memories of visiting the Yekuana was of their smiles and humour. They were easy to get along with and greatly enjoyed the interest we took in their traditions. Luís in particular, who had lived a very traditional life, explained the Yekuana cosmology and how they view their place in the world. He told me that young Yekuana feel ashamed of their traditions because the people they trade with outside their tribal territory look down at them and deride them for their 'primitive beliefs'. This saddened me, for these people have a faith every bit as meaningful and beautiful as any other. They do not force feed it to outsiders and their belief system is tightly bound to their interaction with the forest that is their home. The forest they have every right to feel proud of, nurtured and cared for unlike so much of our wild land. A symbol of the Yekuana connection to nature was an X-shaped blaze in a tree that Luís took me to. More than forty years ago he had cut into that tree to tap it for its latex which he used to fashion a ball to play with. Today, such toys have been replaced by those that must be bought or traded. There was a slight sadness about him as he related this: I felt that for Luís this loss of tradition was

The village chief (centre) flanked by two senior members of the community.

The right piece of wood and his parang were all Benito
needed to make a paddle: 'If you can't make a paddle,
you're not a Yekuana'.

symbolic of a wind of change and
uncertainty that blows through the
forest. But some traditions are still
alive. When I asked him about the
fishing rods I had seen his wife
using, he led me to a long thin
sapling. He cut it down, trimmed
it and then hardened and
straightened it over my fire. I told
Luís that in Britain you can spend
a whole month's wages on a new
fishing rod. He burst out laughing
and said: 'Well, you're throwing
your money away. You can come
here and cut one for nothing.' Such
is the generosity of the Yekuana
and for me it was a lesson in
humanity.

The rivers are the highways and lifelines of the rainforest, but the strong currents and
powerful rapids make them dangerous for the inexperienced. The Yekuana's mastery of these
waterways is immediately apparent in the way they effortlessly negotiate white water. One
morning, while filling my water bottles, I watched a boy of about ten years of age manoeuvre a
canoe upstream with astonishing grace and dexterity. Ten metres long and extremely heavy, these
craft are well suited to the rigours of the waters on which they float, but are far from easy to
manoeuvre. This didn't deter the young boy, who leapt with confidence into this craft and, using
only a pole and his Yekuana sense of timing, steered it easily against the current and through a
set of rapids with a fluidity of movement matched only by the water itself. This one-ness with
the river stretches beyond mere canoeing ability. The Yekuana have the deepest respect for the
river and never throw rubbish into it. As our canoes glided silently downriver, we were in an
entirely unpolluted environment. The sounds were natural, the air was clean, the crystal-clear
waters were pristine and a constant stream of yellow butterflies rose and fell along the bank.

Before we left Kanarakuni I hoped to see how the Yekuana went about bushcraft's most
fundamental skill: lighting a fire. Eight years earlier I had seen the neighbouring Sanema tribe
use a hand drill for fire-starting. I asked Benito and Saul if they would show me. After a search
of several days they collected together the wood they needed and Benito and Saul prepared to
demonstrate. But almost as soon as they began it became apparent that they had never seen the
method. It was, to say the least, an embarrassing moment, for the Yekuana take a great pride in
their skills. With trepidation – and relying on the depth of friendship that had developed

between us – I asked if they would like me to show them how. Fully prepared for a proud rebuke, I was astonished when they said 'Yes'. My experience told me that although the wood they had collected would work, I guessed that the knowledge of *how* had fallen victim to newer, more convenient ways. Working together we swiftly fashioned drill and hearth. Without access to suitable tinder, I raided the BBC medical kit for a field dressing for a less-than-ideal tinder bundle, and fire was kindled. I asked them how far they had to travel to buy matches, but never expected the reply which came: 'Nineteen days by canoe'! Over the next two days we worked together to find suitable tinder and Benito and Saul practised at every spare moment, because it was important for them to be able to make this fire for themselves before we left. The last thing we filmed, at their request, was Benito and Elilio, representing the next generation, making a fire. A skill had returned, pride was restored and independence was renewed.

There is no denying that some traditions are dying out among the Yekuana, but the resourcefulness and skills of the older generation, in particular, are still impressive. When you see a Yekuana in his own environment he is king. To see him away from it is depressing. Today forest Indians from many tribes are lured to the cities in search of wealth but are unprepared for life in the outside world, and unable to find their way home. Lost and exploited they wander the streets of Caracas and other cities, unemployed and despised by an alien society of which they have no understanding.

It is astonishing with what careless abandon the accumulated wisdom and cultural heritage of peoples like the Yekuana is discarded in the path of 'progress'. For the time being their sheer remoteness and the Venezuelan government help to protect their way of life. All over the world rainforest is under pressure from logging, mining and other industries. Almost certainly, the next hundred years will see the passing of the hunter-gatherer way of life. Whether this is a good thing or a bad thing is not the debate we should be having. More important, I believe, is to find ways to protect their specialised environmental understanding so they can teach those born into cultures which long ago lost such wisdom. People like the Yekuana live in a harmony with their environment that outsiders can only envy. It is not a question of the ancient world versus the modern world: it is about blending our technology with traditional wisdom.

From hand drill (1) to glowing ember (2) to smoke (3) to a proper blaze! Whatever a person's age, firemaking is always fascinating. This skill has a real value when you live nineteen days by canoe from the nearest place to buy matches.

All along the river, clouds of butterflies dance over the shingle.

The Lost World
of the Pemon

Spiders' webs like these are to be seen everywhere in the jungle.

I love living and travelling in the jungle but I have always been wary of falling too deep under its enchanting spell. The hypnotic beauty of its sights, sounds and smells is matched only by the myriad hazards that lurk at every turn. To live and travel in deep jungle requires not only a good knowledge of this very particular environment but also a range of practical skills and crafts which allow you to make the most of the abundance of natural materials to hand. In short, the jungle-trekker needs to be versed in the ancient art of bushcraft. Living in a tropical rainforest, however, need not be a case of mere survival. It is possible to live there in genuine comfort, so long as we follow the rules of the jungle.

After our week with the Yekuana we set off on a traditional trading route which for centuries has linked that ancient group of people to another, the Pemon, who live right on the edge of the rainforest where the land turns to savannah. It is imperative to travel as light as possible in a rainforest, where there are many natural obstacles and where the heat and humidity are merciless in sapping your energy. This was not a lesson heeded by the planners of a disastrous jungle expedition by a group of American scientists back in 1923. The farcical nature of that journey is recorded in a book called *White Waters and Black* by explorer Gordon McCreagh who, speculation has it, was the inspiration for the Hollywood character Indiana Jones. The expedition to the Amazon was the most expensive ever undertaken and – supposedly – it was also the best equipped. But it ended in abject failure and bitter recrimination. Outdoor equipment has changed dramatically for the better over the years, but even by the standards of the early twentieth century the amount of kit taken on this venture was ludicrously excessive. In total there were four tonnes of equipment, much of it packed into heavy cases, and at one stage the team's mule train stretched as far as four miles.

As they headed into the jungle, the expedition quickly began to fall apart under the weight of pressures which they had brought upon themselves.

Home in the forest: travellers must come prepared with modern lightweight materials to create a small haven from frequent tropical downpours.

The infighting was bitter, several of the group leaders quit the venture prematurely and the team returned home with virtually no scientific findings of any worth. The hapless botanist was so busy inventing animal sightings for a book which he hoped would make his name and fortune that he did not realise McCreagh and the entomologist were feeding him false sightings of animals that lived in entirely different parts of the world.

Sensible planning, light equipment and practicality are the keys to a successful jungle journey. One of the fundamental rules is to give yourself a reasonable amount of time before nightfall to set up camp. It is of the greatest importance to find the right site where you will be as safe as possible from potential hazards. Over the years I have drawn up a mental checklist when I am preparing to bed down for the night in the rainforest. The first thing I do is look for two trees the right distance apart for a hammock and then I check to make sure there are no dead branches overhead. 'Widow-makers', as they are known, need only be small branches to cause serious damage when they fall from a great height. Next, using your machete, you should always clear small saplings from the ground underneath your hammock area, so that no unwelcome creatures can crawl up to pay you a visit in the night. I also make sure there are no wasp nests in the immediate area before taking a branch and sweeping away all the leaf matter from the campsite to eradicate the risk of encountering scorpions and biting centipedes. If there are fallen trees, or a pile of logs and branches, give them a poke with a long stick as a further precaution.

One of the things I love about travelling through jungles is the way a patch of rainforest can be transformed into home by the simple act of putting up your hammock. You need to know just three knots to set up your camp, all of them quick-release to make it easy for you to pack up and go at first light. I always pack my hammock in a 'dry bag' so that even if I fall into a river I know that I will have a good comfortable night ahead of me.

If it is raining when you stop for the night, it is always sensible first of all to tie up your waterproof sheet (the 'tarp') above the hammock area to protect you from the elements as you go about preparing the rest of the site. Once the hammock is tied up – which should take a matter of seconds rather than minutes – all you need is your travel pillow and a poncho liner and you are ready to settle down for the night. It is one of the great pleasures of jungle travel to light a fire before going to bed. This not only keeps the bugs away and provides some light, it also provides a comforting focus around which fellow travellers can unite at the end of a hard day's trek.

The way you pack camp away is actually more important than the way you pitch it because you want everything to be in a neat, logical order, so that when you are tired and soaked with sweat and the light is starting to fade rapidly, you can remove your rucksack and quickly establish base for the night. What you do not want to be doing is emptying your whole rucksack in the rain to find the waterproof tarpaulin at the bottom. The tarp should always go in the top of the rucksack because it is the first thing you need when you come to set up camp. Nor do you want to find yourself standing in the gathering darkness quickly trying to disentangle a bird's nest of strings and lines attached to your equipment. It is this sort of attention to detail that makes all the difference in bushcraft. There is also a great sense of satisfaction to be derived from this type of well-drilled routine and taking responsibility for your own comfort and well-being day after day.

Today it is possible to travel through the jungle in relative comfort, but there were few physical consolations and little relief for the intrepid explorers of the Victorian Age. During the nineteenth century there was a rush of British and other western scientists and adventurers to the most remote corners of the globe as they sought to discover and understand the mysteries of the natural world. Some important studies and great works of research were produced in this period and high among those achievements is *The Naturalist on the River Amazon* by Henry Bates. Bates is perhaps best known for his theory on mimicry, observing that many species would mimic the colour of poisonous ones to avoid being eaten by predators. What I like particularly about Bates's book is his almost tangible love of the jungle, which he described as a place of permanent summer where growth has gone mad. He wrote:

In these tropical forests each plant and tree seems to be striving to outgrow its fellow, struggling upwards towards light and air, branch and leaf and stem regardless of its neighbours. It is especially the enjoyment of life, manifested by individual existences, which compensates for the destruction and pain caused by the inevitable competition.

When we emerged from the jungle on our way to visit the Pemon we were met with what must surely be one of the most breathtaking natural scenes on the entire planet. Before us lay a landscape of massive, steep-sided mountains known as the Tepuís, many of which have vast table-top plateaus at their summit. (The whole of Greater London could fit on the biggest of the Tepuís.) To the Pemon, the Tepuís are where their gods live, just as Mount Olympus was to the Greeks in classical times. These mountains in the Guiana Highlands on the Venezuela/Brazil border are so old that they even predate life on earth, as no fossils have ever been found in them. Because they are so steep and difficult to climb, they have remained largely unexplored over the years, thus adding to the sense of deep mystery that has always enveloped them.

Sir Arthur Conan Doyle's novel *The Lost World*, written in 1912, tells the story of the discovery of dinosaurs on top of a remote mountain. The book was said to have been inspired by a lecture he attended at the Royal Geographical Society in which the first Europeans to climb a Tepuí, Everard Im Thurn and Harry H. Perkins, transfixed their audience with the account of their experiences. One of the Tepuís, known as Auyán, is home to the highest waterfall on earth, Angel Fall, which is almost a kilometre high and took its name from an American pilot and adventurer in the 1930s called Jimmy Angel who discovered it. Like many before him, Angel was certain that he had spotted gold on top of a Tepuí from his plane, but he crashed when he attempted a landing on the uneven surface. Somehow Angel survived the impact and managed to walk to safety. No gold was ever found but his daring exploit earned him such fame that years later his plane was lifted off the Tepuí by helicopter and it now stands outside the airport in the city of Ciudad Bolivar.

It would be another half a century or so before the invention of the satellite phone and the revolutionary Global Positioning System (GPS) –

two essential pieces of equipment, in my judgement, when travelling through still largely unmapped regions of the planet like the Amazon. Whether using the phone for an emergency, or to call for helicopter logistics support, or simply to contact someone back home, communication by satellite has revolutionised the way we can travel and explore.

In this age of cutting-edge technology it is hard for us to imagine the difficulties endured by some of the earliest visitors to this region. The incredible story of Isabela Godin and her French husband, Jean, provides a dramatic illustration of the navigation and communication problems facing earlier generations.

Isabela was a native of Peru who met her husband in the headwaters of the Amazon, where she lived. He embarked on an attempt to measure the circumference of the earth in 1749. By the time the job was over the couple had two children and were expecting a third. Isabela stayed in the Amazon while Jean set off to arrange passage home to France. Ten years later her husband had still not returned and during that period she had suffered the anguish of watching her children die of disease.

When she heard rumours that a boat sent to collect her was somewhere in the region, she set off with a party of several dozen others to find it. Indeed there was a boat, but her trials were far from over for when she arrived at a village which had been destroyed by smallpox, her crew deserted her. Undeterred, she and a handful of surviving villagers set off downriver in an old battered canoe on an epic journey, travelling for over one thousand miles through the meandering tributaries of the largest river system on earth. The rest of her party died one by one, leaving Isabela with no choice but to try to walk out of the forest on her own. No one knows how far she walked and we can only imagine the horrific ordeal she must have endured. Incredibly, she survived the experience and a full twenty years after they parted she and her husband were finally reunited in 1770.

I am pleased to say that we had no such trouble locating the Pemon community in the village of Yunek on our expedition to the region. I knew we were getting close to our destination as we headed out of the forest and into the savannah, because every now and then we came across an area which had been burned to the ground in order to encourage new growth. The young shoots of the scorched area attracted animals and thus made it easier for the Pemon to hunt them.

At our final site before arriving in Yunek, we had an amusing moment while we were busy setting up camp and getting the camera equipment ready for filming when two men emerged from the woods carrying bows and arrows. They stared at us and we stared at them. They couldn't speak our language and we couldn't speak theirs because we had no translator with us at that point, but there was mutual fascination and an urge to communicate with each other. It was clear they had never seen television equipment before, and they were also curious about our modern-style hammocks which were so different from their own. To understand how odd this encounter must have been for them, imagine going into the woods at the end of your garden and discovering a group of South American Indians setting up their camp for the night.

The village of Yunek is one of the most beautiful places I have ever visited and although it has a timeless air about it, I was taken aback by how heavily influenced the villagers had become by the more modern world beyond. Although there is still no running water – they wash and drink from the river – the community owned a village video camera. Throughout the village there was clear evidence of how traditional bushcraft skills had gone into decline; with every acquisition of a modern tool or piece of equipment, a little piece of Pemon culture had been lost. The construction of their traditional dwellings, however, is one area of Pemon life where you can still see their ancient bushcraft skills in operation. These homes illustrate perfectly the place where they live, on the border of two entirely different environments; the roofs and structure of the buildings are made from wood and palm leaves cut from the jungle, while the walls are finished with earth from the savannah.

One interesting fact we learned was that the palm leaves are never to be cut during a full moon, as its gravitational influence means the leaves retain more water and are therefore liable to rot sooner. Cutting these branches efficiently demands considerable skill with a machete or parang, the single most valuable bushcraft tool in this environment. A machete is as versatile as the person using it but it is important to keep it in its sheaf until you need it, because it will bite you as fast as it will bite the wood if given half a chance. A sharp machete and a sound technique allow you to gather what you need very quickly, which is important when you are working in a highly humid climate that drains you of strength so swiftly.

The men of Yunek tend to work in bursts, as and when there is a task that needs carrying out, such as constructing a new building in the village, or clearing away an area of forest to create a garden in which they can grow their fruit and vegetables. Cotton and manioc have been a mainstay of Pemon life over the years, but the earth on the edge of the savannah does not make farming easy and it is more a question of eking out a subsistence. (The pineapples we were given by our hosts

Both the Yekuana and the Pemon clear areas of the forest to grow crops.

were the best I have ever tasted, however.) The land in which they live may be beautiful, but it is not bountiful and the Pemon have had to develop highly sophisticated bushcraft skills over the centuries in order to live off it. The poor quality of the land for growing crops and grazing cattle is the main reason why the Pemon survived the incursions of settlers and farmers and were able to maintain their ancient way of life for so much longer than other aboriginal people of the Amazon region.

Traditionally the Pemon are semi-nomadic people, living a 'slash-and-burn' existence: when they had exhausted the natural resources of the area, the whole community would uproot and settle down at a new location and start afresh. That way of life has been complicated since the Christian

missionaries arrived in the area and set about trying to establish permanent communities with a school, a church, a clinic and other 'modern' institutions. The forest cannot support people for long if they stay in the same place and, unable to live with the land as they had done in the past, the villagers have come to rely more heavily on the world outside at the expense of their traditional way of life.

Many of the ancient South American peoples have been lured towards the cities and towns in search of work and money, but often this has ended in disaster for those who make the break from home. Disorientated by their unfamiliar urban surroundings and often looked down upon by the city-dwellers, many of the Indians become lost souls and fall into a life of poverty and destitution. When I was with the Yekuana the week before some of the older men told me that when they go out of the forest, people laugh at them because they worship the sun. Not wanting to feel excluded or even stranger in an alien environment, the Yekuana youngsters often abandon or disown their traditional beliefs. The tragedy, or injustice, is that these people have lived with these belief systems for thousands of years without damaging the environment or forcing their philosophy of life on other people. In my view, we should have much greater respect for these ancient belief systems.

There is no Pemon word for 'year' and instead they refer to two separate times of year: wet and dry. There are no seasons and no harvest time as their crops are grown continuously. In the drier periods, the Pemon clear their plots for cultivation traditionally with axes and machetes, cutting the trees into the centre of a plot so that when they burn the cleared area, the fire does not spread into the wider forest. After the burning, heavy loads of manioc plants are brought from the old plots, usually by the women using fibre backpacks. Manioc is the staple of the Pemon diet and it is used to make flour for bread and also crushed into a paste for the brewing of a powerful beer. The manioc root does not yield its goodness easily and it is a laborious process for the community's women to remove all its poison and convert it into a nutritious foodstuff. After the roots are dug up and carried back to the village, they have to be grated, squeezed, peeled and dried before they can be prepared for eating.

The roles of Pemon men and women have always been clearly defined, but whereas the females worked continuously either in the fields, spinning cotton or making hammocks, the males worked sporadically, hunting, fishing or clearing the forest. But the Pemon do not have an equivalent

Tepuí, the extraordinary rock formations that inspired such works as *The Land That Time Forgot* and *The Lost World*. Often only accessible by air, they have a unique ecosytem.

word for 'work' in their vocabulary because the tasks they have to perform are seen as a part of daily life rather than something distinct. It has been many decades, though, since the Pemon have lived a self-sufficient life and their households today are a mixture of traditional and modern 'outside' items. The signs of creeping modernisation are everywhere in Yunek: the youngsters play football constantly, most of them wear T-shirts bearing the names of western products and disco music blares out from modern hi-fi equipment.

In my view, there is no point in bemoaning the wearing away of ancient cultures such as that of the Pemon people. You cannot preserve in aspic these traditional ways of life for the sake of your own enjoyment or appreciation. Societies and cultures are constantly evolving and nothing can stop the momentum of historical change. Time does not sit still, even for aboriginal communities living in the remotest areas of the world. We should

leave people to determine their own destiny and not tell others how to live their lives. If a man finds that an outboard motor is more efficient than a traditionally crafted wooden paddle, then we have to accept that as a fact of progress. I prefer to admire and learn from what remains of these ancient communities – especially their bushcraft skills – while they still exist.

When I made a short journey to see some nearby rock paintings shortly before bidding our Pemon hosts farewell, I was reminded that while the modern world has encroached deep into their life, their past will never be entirely eradicated. Standing on that site, I felt a powerful connection with the past, as I always do when I encounter aboriginal art. These paintings would have been created before the Pemon had any contact with the outside world and ancient superstition and myths still surround them.

As I explored the area, my sense of the past coming to life was compounded by the discovery of evidence of other human activity. Much of the ground had been scorched by camp fires and I also found the remains of an old stone blade that had clearly been worked upon with another stone. Curiously, there were also pieces of quartz and jasper at the site and as neither of these materials is found locally, they must have been acquired through trade with people from outside the region – either that, or they were brought there by the outsiders themselves.

I find it thrilling that through one small archaeological artefact like the piece of a blade, the smear of some red ochre on a wall or a lump of charcoal, you can experience a powerful sensation of a world deep in the distant past, a world where the inhabitants had nothing to rely upon but their bushcraft skills in order to survive and flourish.

Pemon rock art

Whenever I think about my visit to the Amazon, it is the sense of space I remember: it would be a tragedy if the encroachment of 'civilisation' ever destroys the feeling of true wilderness.

Camping with the Hadza

Some of the great explorers have described the experience of setting foot on African soil as a sense of coming home. Whenever I return to that magical continent, I always feel an overwhelming connection with the past, a powerful sensation of returning to my very distant roots.

Reunited with my old friend, Gudo.

It was in Africa that mankind's long journey through evolution began and it was there that man first began to work out how to use the natural world around him to his advantage. That is what bushcraft is all about: understanding our environment and living by its gifts.

As part of my last visit there I went to meet the Hadza of northern Tanzania, who are amongst the last remaining hunter-gatherer tribes on earth. To them bushcraft is a way of life, although their ancient culture has become increasingly vulnerable to the forces of modernisation in recent years. The Hadza live for the present, taking each day as it comes, never storing or preserving their food. The vast majority have never seen a doctor or stepped inside a school. The men of this nomadic tribe roam the vast open plains and the forested shores of Lake Eyasi, using powerful bows and arrows to hunt a variety of animals including antelope, buffalo, bush baby, rabbit, bird and occasionally even lion, leopard, giraffe and hyena. The Hadza eat everything they kill and use other parts of the animal for a variety of purposes. Giraffe neck tendons, for instance, are used as string for their bows. The Hadza women, meanwhile, scour the land for berries, seeds, roots, honey and fruit from the magnificently versatile baobab tree.

Our journey took us through Arusha, the capital of Northern Tanzania and then west to Karatu, the last significant township before we headed out into the largely uninhabited plains. On my last excursion to the vibrant marketplace of Karatu it took the better part of a day to get there as we slid and bumped along the muddy, pot-holed road, but the route had since been tarmacked and this time the journey took just two hours. The new freeway was further evidence, if it was needed, of the modern world's relentless expansion into every corner of the planet, shrinking wildernesses as it goes. The best African markets are wonderful, colourful places brimming with fresh fruit and vegetables, as well as an extraordinary assortment of goods made from recycled materials. When you see these ingeniously assembled items you realise that the African gift for recycling virtually everything in their possession is something we could learn from in the west.

After stocking up with provisions from the market we headed further west towards our Hadza encampment. As the main road turned into a dust track, I had that tremendous feeling I always get when I leave the modern world behind and disappear into an ancient wilderness, far away from the well-beaten tourist routes. When I take a trip to this sort of climate and environment I like to travel even lighter than I normally do and keep the camp as simple and uncluttered as possible. Without the distraction and mess of equipment on site, you engage far more quickly and intimately with your surroundings. I could have used a tent, but I prefer to live in a fly camp with just a big

Women digging for edible roots which they cook in the embers of the fire (above). They have a very detailed knowledge of the flora and are alert to every seasonal glut. I am a great admirer of the simplicity of Hadza life.

Tubers are cooked on a small fire to provide a
nourishing and tasty meal. Their cooking methods are
reduced to a sophisticated simplicity.

Typical scenes of Hadza life: they are very keen archers and spend a lot of time making arrows, which you can see drying in the trees on the right.

tarpaulin sheet over my head and my whole world underneath it. You can get some very lightweight tarps these days, but on this particular trip we had vehicle support and so I was able to take an old-fashioned heavy canvas which has a degree of solidity that the nylon flysheet lacks.

I never feel at home on a campsite until the campfire is going, but in an area where firewood is relatively hard to come by, I always make sure the fire is a modest one. In many parts of the world, local people have to go to a lot of effort to collect firewood and they do not like to see visitors wasting their precious commodity in a giant blaze. A good shovel is another essential piece of equipment for this sort of camping and ideally it should have a solid metal handle to cope with the African soil which has been baked hard by the sun. You can use the shovel for a number of different purposes including digging your latrine, moving embers from the fire for cooking and, should the need arise, to deter predators from taking too close an interest in the campsite. Hyenas have been known to bite off people's faces as they slept.

The only other indispensable items of kit you need for the fly camp are a bedroll and a mosquito net which should be tightly tucked in to keep out any curious insects. The fly camp is not just very simple to set up, it also has a lovely sense of space and freedom which you do not get when you are confined in a tent. You also get plenty of shade from the sun and a good cool breeze as well as a 360-degree panorama of your surroundings. The fly camp would not be a sensible choice in an area teeming with big game, but even in less dangerous areas you should always have a fire going to keep predators at bay. It is also sensible to bed down at a reasonable hour as sleep is difficult once the sun has started its early morning ascent. On this occasion, however, it was rain and not sun that roused me from a deep sleep on our first night in camp. It was the start of the rainy season in East Africa and at four o'clock in the morning the heavens opened and the rain hammered and rattled on my tarpaulin like hail on a tin roof.

I had spent a wonderful time with the Hadza eight years earlier and I was especially curious to discover whether their way of life had changed at all since then. The settlement we visited that morning was a typical Hadza camp – not so much a village as a very temporary home, featuring a handful of huts made of grass and sticks which are put up by the women of the community in just a couple of hours. One of the features I love most about the Hadza is that they have virtually no material possessions and that allows them to move around their world with ease. They are the original light travellers. They are also constantly on the move and there is very little clutter or dirt in the sites where they choose to settle.

One of the Hadza I was most keen to be reunited with was a very interesting character called Mustafa, who was learning about herbalism on my last visit here and who was now very knowledgeable in his field. There is little that Mustafa does not know about the uses for all the plants in his area and he gave me a brief introduction to his specialised subject. After demonstrating how the Hadza treat ear infections, he showed me another plant which they take if they are bitten by a poisonous snake, chewing the root to induce vomiting and diarrhoea in order to flush the poison from the system. Mustafa told me he had been bitten by two of Africa's most poisonous snakes, the black mamba and the green mamba, and on each occasion he survived because he had chewed the roots.

The following day, at first light, the Hadza women invited me to see how they gather food from the bush. Watching these highly professional fruit-pickers at work was a sight to behold as they set about gathering the

community's provisions for the day. First we watched them climb trees to collect some berries called ndushibi, which are a very sticky, sweet fruit with a large stone in the middle. Next they were collecting birds' eggs and digging up roots of the sumoko plant which are packed full of energy-giving carbohydrate. Digging is the easy part of the task – it is spotting the vine-like plants and distinguishing them from similar-looking growths which is the difficult bit. You or I would struggle to make the distinction without a close inspection of the different plants, but with their sharp eyes and years of experience the Hadza women were able to recognise what they were looking for without great effort or scrutiny.

The Hadza use a great variety of plants but the baobab tree is especially important to them. The trees, which are found on the African and Indian savannah near the Equator, grow up to twenty-five metres high and have very thick trunks and a wild tangle of branches. Virtually every part of this highly versatile tree is put to some use or other by the Hadza. The trees are leafless for the nine dry months of the year but during the rainy season the Hadza pick the leaves and cook them into a spinach-like mulch. The leaves are also put to medicinal purposes and the bark can be used for making cloth and rope, while the fruit, also known as 'monkey bread', is a staple of the Hadza diet when available. To see them

Food gathering with the Hadza is always fascinating.
Ndushibi berries form a large part of the Hadza diet, but
they also look out for birds' eggs and any other sources
of food. You can learn so much from them and see how
we once lived.

Music is important to the Hadza: Gudo is playing a traditional instrument in the entrance to this ancient baobab tree. The tree has a special significance to the Hadza: within the hollow interior is a large enough space for a woman to give birth. She remains there with the child until the umbilical cord withers away.

through the long dry months, the trees absorb great quantities of moisture during the rainy season, and when the Hadza are thirsty they sometimes cut out little sections of the inner bark and suck the moisture from them. The trunks of the baobab are so big that people often live inside them for a period or use them to take shelter from the elements. The tree we visited also turned out to be the local maternity ward for it was there, we were told, that all the Hadza women came to give birth. One of the women with us had given birth to all nine of her children there, each time staying in the tree for a month until the umbilical cord had fallen off.

It was difficult to imagine during our stay with the Hadza and the Masai in their beautiful surroundings that this region was once the scene of some of the bloodiest fighting of World War One. The campaign waged between Allied troops (made up mainly of British, Indian and white South Africans) and German forces was played out on the furthest fringes of the Great War, largely unnoticed at the time and forgotten since, but it was a remarkable conflict nonetheless.

While their comrades were bogged down in muddy trenches in northern France, the troops found themselves drawn into a far more mobile form of combat – the cat-and-mouse manoeuvres of guerrilla warfare. It was a form of engagement, it turned out, for which the British troops were hopelessly ill-equipped and untrained. This backwater war was dominated by the genius of the German commander, Colonel Paul von Lettow Vorbeck, whose knowledge of the terrain and local conditions allowed him to run rings around his enemy, despite being outnumbered by almost ten to one. Lettow Vorbeck's total force never exceeded more than 14,000, of whom 3,000 were German and 11,000 were Askari (native African) troops. After routing the British troops at the Battle of Tanga Bay, Lettow Vorbeck spent the rest of the war launching dozens of raids across the British territories in Kenya and Zimbabwe (then Southern Rhodesia), and Tanzania (then Tanganyika), tying down over 100,000 troops which would otherwise have been deployed on the Western Front or in the Middle East.

The key to Lettow Vorbeck's success was the bushcraft skills of his Askari troops, who understood how to survive in that environment. While the British were dying in their thousands of dysentery and other diseases, the Askari and Germans generally remained fit, healthy, well-fed and appropriately equipped, by using the

Gudo shows his scars from a leopard attack: most of the older men bear the scars of their encounters with lions, leopards or buffaloes.

95

Ancient rock art created by the Hadza's ancestors. Rites and rituals are still practised by the local villagers on this spot. The giraffe motif is very important in rock art, associated with the coming of rain.

The tell-tale entrance to the nest of the mopane bee.

natural resources under their very noses for sustenance and equipment. The skins of animals killed for food, for instance, were turned into lightweight boots. After the war, Lettow Vorbeck wrote: 'My experience showed me that the German can go barefoot where there are tolerable paths, but never through the bush.'

Following the Askari example, the German troops also plundered the vegetation in order to obtain the nutrients, minerals and vitamins that were vital to their survival. Roots, nuts, berries and a leaf similar to spinach, came to form the staple diet for Lettow Vorbeck's men and helped to keep them in relatively robust health until the end of the conflict. Exploiting every natural resource with a nutritional, medicinal or logistical quality, the Germans were able to toy with their ailing, hapless opponents in the field. The bark of

Raiding the mopane bees' nest to search for honey, a very important source of food.

Eating bushbaby: an animal of any size, no
matter how small, is food to the Hadza,
but they only hunt when they need to eat.

Modern bushcraft has its place: a fresnel lens harnesses the power of the sun to make fire.

trees, for instance, was used as makeshift bandages or stripped into pieces of string to tie up dressings. The Germans also used the sap from certain trees as an effective tool in the fight against malaria. While the Germans used their environment as a kind of natural quartermaster stores-cum-medicine cabinet, the Allies, by contrast, were finding it difficult enough to survive, let alone to form an effective fighting force.

The Armistice was declared on 11 November 1918 but news did not reach Lettow Vorbeck for a further two weeks and he was busy planning his next series of raids when a recently captured British soldier informed him that the war was over. The German commander, then with no more than 3,000 men in his ranks, was obliged to surrender but he was received with a mixture of warmth and awe by the British officers, some of whom admitted they had more affection and respect for this remarkable German than they had for their own leaders.

The Hadza face an uncertain future: I feel privileged to
have travelled and spent time with them.

The Hadza passion for archery starts at an early age: by the time they're fourteen they are able to pull a 100lb bow – not so long ago that would have been the same in Britain.

There can be few communities of people left on earth who depend as heavily on the skills and knowledge of bushcraft as the Hadza. Bushcraft is not so much an occasional activity for this ancient tribe – it is a way of life. As a hunter-gatherer people, bows and arrows are essential to their existence and making them, using materials from the bush, is an important everyday task. A typical Hadza bow is strong, heavy and a little stiff in the pulling action and it is probably not the most impressively crafted weapon I have ever used, but it does its job well enough.

I had brought with me a powerful yew bow made by one of Britain's leading craftsmen to present to them as a gift and make amends for breaking one of theirs when I was last there. I offered it to a character called Gudo, whom I had met in 1997, and was delighted to see the smile on his face when he tried it out. 'It fires like a gun,' he said. I love those moments when I visit different cultures and I find myself bonding over a shared experience, such as shooting an arrow, lighting a fire or tracking an animal with someone who, superficially at least, lives in a world entirely alien to my own. Bushcraft has the power to transcend language and culture boundaries because it gets to the very basics of human existence. It is about using practical skills to survive and subsist in the natural world.

With hunter-gatherers like the Hadza, I have always felt a special sense of kinship, a feeling of communion which I rarely experience with farming people. The simple reason for that I suppose is that while I have never farmed the land, I have always been fascinated by tracking wild animals. Tracking is perhaps the most important bushcraft skill of all and for the Hadza hunters it is crucial to their very existence. The Hadza, many of whom carry scars of their skirmishes with leopards, hunt and eat virtually everything in their environment apart from snakes and other reptiles.

I love the stealth element tracking demands and the thrill of gradually closing in on your target. What other human activity challenges you to use all your senses at once and makes you inspect your natural surroundings with such focus and attention to detail? However, tracking is by no means a stroll in the woods or the bush. Rarely, if ever, are you following lovely clear footprints along a clear, noiseless path with the wind blowing in exactly the right direction. Tracking is very challenging and even the most experienced practitioners often fail to catch up with the animal they have set out to trail. If the wind changes direction, or a twig snaps under your boot, the animal will be gone. We had no luck when we went out with the Hadza, but it was

An ordinary tool like this discarded hand drill I found
outside the giant baobab tree has a special magic: it
forms part of a continuum of fire-lighting knowledge
that stretches back millions of years.

fascinating all the same to watch their techniques in action. At one stage we knew we got close to a leopard, or some other predator, because there was a great deal of activity and disturbance amongst the birds and other animals, but it must have sensed our presence, and quickly disappeared.

There in the woods the Hadza are kings of their world but I could not help but wonder as I watched them go about their daily lives whether their ancient way of life stands on the verge of extinction, as modernisation reaches out and tightens its grasp on the world's few remaining wildernesses. While the neighbouring Masai, a more politically-minded people, have to some extent formalised their bushcraft and made it work in the context of the twenty-first century, the Hadza way of life, with its total dependence on bushcraft, seems more fragile and could quickly disappear under the pressure of forces beyond their control.

The morning we left the Hadza came to dance and sing, so we had an impromptu party: connections like this only come from genuine respect and friendship.

Masai Safari

For most people in the west, the word 'safari' conjures up images of comfortable lodges, gin-and-tonics on the verandah and air-conditioned Land Rovers.

But to the Maasai people of East Africa, 'safari' means something quite different. From the Arabic, via the Swahili, the word means 'to travel' and, for a nomadic people like the Maasai, travel is a highly important part of their life and culture. I have always felt uncomfortable and frustrated when I have found myself cooped up in a vehicle heading through a stunning natural environment such as the great plains and bush of East Africa. The chance of experiencing a true safari, Maasai-style, is something I could only dream about as a young boy when I used to head out into the woods near my home in search of foxes, deer, badgers and stoats – the closest we get to a safari in Britain, I suppose. Thus I felt a great sense of excitement when we set off to Angata Kiti, a very remote region in eastern Tanzania and one of extraordinary natural beauty.

Angata Kiti, which means 'small plain' in Swahili, is an unspoiled valley tucked away in the Gol Mountains, a long way off the beaten safari path taken by most visitors to this region. To get there we travelled through one of the best game reserves in the world, the Serengeti, and it was easy to understand why so many tourists have flocked there in their droves since the late nineteenth century. It is not just the promise of seeing animals in their natural habitat – or killing them, as they used to all those years ago – it is also that the Serengeti happens to be one of the most beautiful natural environments on the planet.

The animals have become so accustomed to tourist vehicles that they no longer run away from them, which is great for those who want to record their experience in photographs. One of the dangers, however, is that some people forget that they are in a wilderness, not in the safety of a zoo, and they become lulled into a false sense of security. Before we set off through the Serengeti on a beautiful, clear morning, the lodge manager told me a story about a tourist to illustrate the point. The manager had gone out for a

Ole Dorop, in characteristic red Maasai cloak, on his farm: goats and cattle are central to Maasai life and culture.

Before we fell asleep, safe within our 'boma', the talk was of women, cattle and ghosts. In truth all human beings are the same and it's a shame we don't celebrate our similarities more, rather than focussing on our differences.

drive a few days before we arrived but had to pull over sharply when, to his alarm, he spotted one of his guests, in full running gear, taking an early morning jog across the plain. He quickly bundled him into the vehicle, saying: 'What do you think you're doing? Feeding the lions?'

Our campsite was in the heart of Masai country, where the rolling hills provide plenty of lush pasture for their cattle. Throughout the year, the Maasai, the largest tribe in Tanzania, travel in small groups and they live almost entirely on the meat and milk of their herds. The guide for my two-day trek through this stunning landscape was a warrior called Mtele, who had an intimate knowledge of the area, and as we were heading into big-game country, we had also arranged for an experienced, armed ranger to travel with us.

Before setting out, each of us prepared our individual supplies for the trip. For Mtele this meant cutting out the lining of a goat's stomach and filling it with the animal's meat and fat before 'vacuum-sealing' it with a small strip of bark and some wooden pegs. His only other equipment was a sword, a spear and a stick to which he attached his pouch of food. Mtele provided a shining example of how to travel light in the wilderness and although my preparations were slightly different, I too had only a modest amount of kit with me. In addition to my ready-prepared rations, I also took a water purifier, which is essential for anyone who is not local, and a sleeping bag because it can get fairly cold under the cloudless skies of Africa.

As we set off across the vast open plain at the start of our real safari I was quickly struck by how different it felt from being in a vehicle. In this land of sweeping panoramas and huge horizons, you enjoy the most honest perspective and the most tangible sensation of its vastness when you are on foot. On that first day Mtele led us through a deserted village where he had once lived with his extended family. These settlements, known as kraals, consist of half a dozen or so huts made from mud and dung, and they are protected from predators by a thick, spiny thornbush fence called a boma. The huts were so natural, they looked almost as though they had grown out of the ground organically without any help or interference from those who came to live in them. The crumbling huts, Mtele told us, had been abandoned when the rains failed and the family was obliged to move on and quite a family it must have been. Polygamy is common among the older men of the Maasai and Mtele's father, we learned, had taken a staggering twenty-two wives who between them had reared a total of sixty-eight children.

Thompson's gazelle

The pattern on the puff adder's scales is perfect camouflage.

Later in the day we began to look for a site to set up camp in good time as night
falls quickly in this region. We were camping Maasai-style which meant no tents or
modern equipment of any description, just the vegetation we could find near our
chosen site. I am always fascinated to see how different cultures go about organising
their camp and this was the first time I had seen how the Maasai sleep safely in the
bush away from the village. You need protection at night from the hyenas and
cheetahs, and other predators that roam this region. Your first line of defence is a
fire, which will also serve as a source of heat, light and general comfort. Wild
animals do not like smoke or fire and they will generally tend to turn tail at the sight
or smell of it. The fire, Mtele explained, is not just a deterrent to predators, but also
a beacon for fellow journeymen in the area which can be seen for miles around.

For tinder we used an old weaver bird's nest and in no time we had a good fire
going and were able to turn our attention to building a 'boma' barrier, complete
with makeshift door, to encircle and keep us safe as we slept. We needed plenty of
wood to construct our barricade but I made sure to gather it carefully, as this was
just the kind of habitat for scorpions and snakes. After building our home for the
night, Mtele unwrapped his pouch of goat and I cooked up my rations before we
exchanged stories around the campfire and lay down for one of the best night's
sleep I had enjoyed in some time.

If I could pass on one small tip to anyone considering a similar safari through

the African wilderness, it would be this: as often as you can, detach yourself from your companions, walk away from your site and let your senses take in the unfamiliar world around you. You need to be only a few feet from the site to be absorbed into the environment as you stand there listening to the chattering of the birds and the insects and watching animals, such as baboons and monkeys, going about their daily business. It is all too easy on this type of journey to get drawn into the human dynamics and dimension of the trip, and there is a risk you may miss out on some unforgettable moments and experiences.

On our second day of trekking I was surprised when Mtele suddenly led us into a huge gorge. Sheer rock faces towered above us and lush vegetation cascaded down its steep shaded walls as we entered this lost world tucked away from the scorching plain. The peace, cool and solemnity of this enchanting place put me in mind of one of Europe's great medieval cathedrals. It was called Olkarien Gorge and, we were told, it is a major breeding place for the griffin vulture, as well as a botanist's dream with dozens of different types of plant which can be put to a variety of uses, including the castor bean plant from which the deadly poison ricin is produced. For decades ricin was used by the secret services of the Eastern Bloc to carry out assassinations and in recent years it has attracted the attention of terrorists. The castor bean is a beautiful plant that grows up to 15 feet high, and although the seeds, and to a lesser extent the leaves, are highly toxic, the stems can be hollowed out and used as drinking straws.

(Above) Hornbill; (below) Baboons in the early-morning sun: they often fall victim to leopards at this time of day.

The gorge was also brimming with great clumps of aloe whose popularity in the west as a treatment for skin problems and digestive disorders has soared over the past decade or so. (The Maasai also use it to treat infections in the eyes of their cattle.) Aloe, a remarkably soothing and useful field dressing, is not only a highly versatile plant but the juice of its fleshy leaves is also incredibly easy to extract. Firstly you remove the thorns on the side and then slice it lengthways down the middle so that it can be peeled apart. Then you simply apply the lovely cool gel to the affected area. Be careful, however, to ensure that it is aloe you are using as there are very similar looking plants which would burn your skin if applied.

The abundance of natural resources we came across on this short trek was remarkable and there was one plant in particular that I was keen to experiment with, a species of succulent cacti known locally as oldupai. The plant grows there in profusion, and it is better known as 'mother-in-law's tongue', a member of the sansevieria genus. For centuries the native peoples of Africa have used the fibres of the plant for making snares and bowstrings. (Just to confuse us even more, the plant goes by a third name of 'bowstring hemp'.) Using a technique shown to me by the Bushmen of the Kalahari, thousands of miles away on the other side of this vast continent, I pounded the plant until the fibres began to appear. The next step is to remove the pulp of the plant with a sharpened stick before hanging the fibres on a bush to dry. Basic bushcraft skills like this, sadly, are rapidly disappearing owing to the wide availability of man-made materials, which is a shame because there is not much effort needed to produce this highly durable and strong fibre. It also has the virtue of being completely biodegradable while the plant from which it is taken grows back quickly.

With the rich vegetation of the gorge, you would

Female vervet monkey with young: you have to get up early and be very observant (and lucky) to capture a moment like this.

A pride of lions on the move just after dawn. They like to use roads because it's easier: there is definitely a lazy streak in the lion.

imagine that finding water would be a simple task. But it is not unless you are a Maasai. Mtele showed us the hiding place where his people have kept a spade for many years so that those travelling through the area had easy access to water when they needed it. Mtele also knew exactly where to start digging. One of the reasons why water is found in reasonable quantities here is that the shade created by the narrowness of the gorge protects it from evaporating under the constant glare of a powerful sun. As I sat down to enjoy a short break and a refreshing drink I watched Mtele make himself a medicinal tea from the root of a plant. It was one of those small moments when you feel an almost tangible connection with the past; a small scene that Mtele's ancestors would have performed in exactly the same way down the centuries. Whereas for me bushcraft is something distinct from my everyday life, for Mtele it *is* his life, just as it was for all of us on this planet in the not too distant past.

I was sad to say goodbye to Mtele and I felt a twinge of envy as I watched him stride off into the African horizon, the master of this wonderful natural world and keeper of its ancient secrets. The harmony he enjoys with his surroundings was not something shared by the droves of big-game hunters who poured into the region in the late nineteenth century and started shooting anything that moved in order to take home the skins or body parts as trophies or to sell them for financial gain. Hunting still takes place in East Africa today. Some of it is officially authorised and controlled, but there is still a big problem with poachers killing animals for the bushmeat trade. There is greater emphasis on conservation nowadays, although the revenue it generates through tourism for African countries is a fraction of that

produced by hunting. There is a difficult balance to strike here because if conservation tourism cannot pay its own way it will fail and the consequences of that could be extremely grave for Africa's endangered wildlife. Personally I have no interest in shooting animals for sport, but equally I would not campaign against it because a lot of good comes from correctly managed hunting establishments.

Only a handful of our ancestors were aware of the evils and dangers of the outright carnage that used to take place in Africa, but one exception to that rule was a remarkable Englishman called Frederick Courtenay Selous who rejected a traditional family career in banking to pursue his great passion, studying wildlife. Selous's interest in the natural world started when he was a schoolboy at Rugby and ended with him becoming a champion of African wildlife who spoke out against the hunters. His insightful observations are captured in the highly detailed drawings that he made of the animals he studied.

The cause he promoted, and the fame that it brought him, attracted the attention of US President Theodore Roosevelt who became fascinated by the world Selous described in his memoirs *African Nature Notes and Reminiscences*. A letter from Roosevelt was the start of a lengthy correspondence between the two men in which they discussed the behaviour of wild animals and exchanged impassioned views on nature in general. Roosevelt's interest in the subject grew to the extent that, at the end of his eight-year presidency in 1909, he asked Selous to arrange what became the largest safari ever undertaken. Accompanied by his son Kermit and a retinue of 300 men, Roosevelt trekked across what was then called British East Africa into the Belgian Congo and back to Khartoum on the Nile. Over 1,000 specimens, including 500 big game were 'collected' during the epic trip, 17 of them lions, 20 rhinoceroses and 11 elephants – and when the giant convoy finally came to an end Roosevelt was able to declare it 'the most noteworthy collection of big animals ever to come out of Africa'. The slaughter was carried out in the name of education and enlightenment – if not their spirit – as all the animals were destined for the Natural History museum of the Smithsonian in Washington.

During my stay in Tanzania I went to meet a man who has spent a life in the bush filming animals for television. Few men have a better understanding of animal behaviour and an ability to capture it on film than Warren Samuels and I was hoping his skills of observation would help us to find some cheetahs. Looking out over a vast expanse of African short-grass

Hazards of the bush: (left, top to bottom) boomslang, gaboon viper, green mamba; (above) Cape buffalo, one of the most dangerous animals of all – to be given a wide berth at all times.

plain that morning, it seemed that we would have to be very lucky to get a glimpse of the world's fastest land animal.

The best time for spotting cheetahs is between sunrise and around nine o'clock, before they seek out the shade of a tree as the heat of the sun intensifies. We were close to giving up hope of a sighting when suddenly a whole family of the cats strolled into view in the distance. Seeing two adults together is a rare enough sight in itself, but in a few awesome seconds we were also treated to the spectacle of one of them accelerating to 70 mph and bringing down an unsuspecting Thompson gazelle grazing nearby. Watching one of the most majestic creatures on earth making a kill was a breathtaking sight that will remain vivid in my memory for ever.

This world in which the cheetah lives is under constant threat and its population has been shrinking for over a hundred years. In 1900 it was estimated that there were over 100,000 cheetahs in Africa. Today there are thought to be between 10,000 and 15,000. Hunting has long since been made illegal but the threat from poachers in pursuit of huge profits on the black market will never go away. At the end of our trip to East Africa we hopped over the Tanzanian border to meet some members of the Kenyan Wildlife Service which leads the field in protecting this ancient natural heritage for future generations. Before the KWS was founded in 1988 an estimated 5,000 elephants a year were being poached for their ivory. Extinction

Men of the legendary Kenya Wildlife Service with some of the ivory they have confiscated from poachers, who are often heavily armed.

was a near-certainty. Fifteen years later, that has all changed, thanks in large part to the 2,000-strong force of rangers who roam the vast expanses of the bush tracking down the criminals. The ivory trade has all but died out and elephant numbers are growing again.

The rangers of the KWS are regarded with awe by the Kenyan public and by other members of the country's military and security services. They are a highly trained body of men who use a combination of modern equipment and the traditional skills of the outdoorsman to weed out the poachers and protect the wildlife in the area. The ancient bushcraft skill of tracking, a skill which has fascinated me since childhood, is one at which the rangers excel and I needed little persuasion to go and see them in action.

The area in which they have to operate covers hundreds of square miles and picking up a trail is a major challenge. Most tracking involves the search for animals but the task of the Kenyan rangers is to root out people. The principles and techniques involved, however, are broadly similar. To get an idea of how they go about their work, one of our television crew, together with an armed ranger to protect her from possible attack by a cape buffalo, set off into the bush. We chose a reasonably challenging terrain, consisting of a mixture of lush vegetation and hard rock, and it was fascinating to see them picking up the tell-tale signs of our 'fugitives'.

What struck me most about their incredible expertise was that their skills were not based on hi-tech modern gadgetry but on an ancient knowledge of bushcraft. If I needed conclusive proof of the relevance of bushcraft in the modern world, the rangers of the Kenyan Wildlife Service provided it as emphatically as a footprint in the sand.

The Maasai have an extraordinarily deep knowledge of plants – not just as food or medicine. They know which plant will produce a soap-like substance: it's this kind of mundane knowledge that is most easily lost.

While I was in the area I was also honoured to be invited to an extremely special place, known as the Olpul, where ancient Maasai traditions are passed on from one generation to the next. Few westerners are welcomed here and I felt very privileged to visit this inner sanctum of their culture. This spiritual place is a long way from the village, hidden away in a deep ravine, and the young men of the tribe who have reached a certain age stay there for days, even weeks at a time, absorbing the knowledge and wisdom of their elders.

The goat plays an important role in this rites-of-passage retreat, providing the food to sustain the Maasai men during their stay. I am always moved by the deep respect many indigenous people show for the animals they live alongside and upon which they depend for their food. On this occasion I observed a poignant scene in which they smothered their goat in a curiously dignified way. Watching the young Maasai drinking the blood and tasting the meat of their freshly slaughtered animal may not appeal to western sensibilities but it is a key moment in a young Masai's initiation into manhood.

Using the spear to protect their cattle, as well as themselves and their homesteads from predators, is one of the most important skills that the young Maasai are taught as they grow up. Until recently, the young men – or 'warriors' as the Maasai call them – had to display their prowess with the spear in an elaborate and dangerous initiation ceremony in which they hunted and killed a lion. Today, however, they would only kill a lion if they were in danger. One man who witnessed young Maasai fighting lions was an Englishman called Sir Harry Johnston, who was fascinated by what was then called British Central Africa, and during his various explorations and studies in the late nineteenth century, he made the earliest recordings of

Young Maasai take great pride in personal adornment – it's an important phase in the transition to manhood.

their voices and their songs. We reproduced some of Harry Johnston's recordings and played them to our Maasai hosts to see how much they were able to understand. It was heart-warming to discover that there was instant recognition of what they heard, proving that, for the time being at least, the Masai are succeeding in keeping alive their ancient traditions.

The Olpul, heart of Maasai culture, is not only a kind of school and place of initiation but also a retreat from the tensions of village life. Long may this ancient African tradition continue.

Ole Dorop shares his wisdom with a new generation including his son (left, in purple cloak). Part of the Maasai teaching is how to stay safe when living among predators. They learn only to kill in self-defence and only to kill with a spear when necessary.

The Making of
the *Goosefeather*

Becky Mason
Daughter of the legendary canoeist Bill Mason, Becky is recognised in her own right for her canoeing prowess and her promotion of canoeing in the context of wilderness conservation.

The birch tree is probably the most useful of all the trees and its gifts to humankind are celebrated in folklore wherever it grows. Here in Canada our task was to make a birch-bark canoe, working with Pinock Smith, an Algonquin Indian canoe builder whose knowledge has descended directly from the master canoe builders of the past. Our canoe would be built quickly – as the elders remember them being made – in only a few days. This would not be a fancy showboat, but a craft made with only the traditional tools of axe, crooked knife and awl. One day while we were working a goose swam past, leaving a feather floating in the water. So now our canoe had a name: *Nika Migwan – Goosefeather.*

Kirk Whipper
Canoeist, environmentalist and founder of the Canadian Canoe Museum, Kirk Whipper received the Order of Canada for his pioneering efforts to preserve Canada's canoe heritage.

Splitting cedar logs into planks

With axe and wedge, cedar logs are quartered to more manageable proportions, and then they are split to size by hand. Easy to split, light in weight and resistant to decay, cedar is a key component in the Algonquin canoe.

Rough-hewing the gunwales and inwales

The longest pieces of cedar in the canoe are the gunwales. These are first split out and then rough-hewn to shape. Two extra pieces are produced in case of breakages.

Shaving down the gunwales and inwales with a crooked knife

The rough-hewn gunwales are now tidied and properly shaped using the woodland Indians' most unique tool – the crooked knife.

Lashing ends of temporary inwales with rawhide

The ends of the temporary inwales are lashed together with rawhide

The temporary inwales

Pulled apart in this way, the temporary inwales give the first indication of the shape of the canoe we are building.

The temporary inwales and temporary thwarts

To maintain this shape, temporary thwarts of cedar are tied in place. This frame will set the shape of the finished canoe.

Laying down the birch bark

On ground which has been specially levelled and cleaned of twigs and stones, the sheet of birch bark is unrolled with the white outer layer of bark uppermost. This will eventually become the inside of the canoe.

Placing on the temporary inwales

The frame made by the temporary inwales is laid centrally on the bark sheet.

Shaping temporary sheeting

Temporary sheeting of thin boards is split and shaped from cedar and laid on top of the frame like decking.

Inwales and temporary sheeting weighted down with rocks

On top of this decking heavy river boulders are laid to weight it down.

Folding up the sides of the bark
Around the outside of the frame the bark is bent upwards.

Cutting gores
To enable the bark to be folded evenly upwards all around the frame, slits called gores must be made to allow the bark to overlap in places and prevent bulging.

Sides staked on outside
As the bark is bent upwards and starts to take on the required shape, it is secured with upright posts.

Sides staked on inside

To prevent the bark curling over, more stakes are now carefully placed inside the outer stakes. These have flattened tips like a screwdriver so that they can be slid between the inside of the bark and the outside of the gunwale frame. The inner and outer stakes are then tied together.

Carving pegs

Small pencil-like pegs are now carved from cedar: these will be used to hold together the components of the canoe in a method reminiscent of birch-bark basket construction.

Extra sections of bark added

At the middle section of the bark, extra sections of bark are fitted into place
to allow an even gunwale line. These are secured with temporary battens of
cedar which are slipped between the upright stakes.

Soaking the spruce root lacing

While this is taking place, long spruce roots are soaking
in the lake. These are now split lengthways to form neat
flat lacing.

Bark additions pegged together

The extra pieces of bark are now
pegged in place. First, holes are
drilled using a simple awl, and then
the cedar pegs are used to pin the
pieces together.

Bark additions laced together

The bark sections are now neatly laced into position.

Support for inwales

With hands tired from root stitching, the inwales proper are fitted into place with simple temporary supports. At this stage the depth of the canoe is established, with allowance for the fact that the finished canoe will be set deeper than it looks at the moment.

Outwale and inwale pegged together

With the height of the inwale established, the proper outwale can now be fitted in place. This is done by using an awl to drill holes through the outwale, bark and inwale, and then pegging them together.

147

Outwale and inwale laced together

Once it is held together with the pegs, the protruding ends of the pegs can be cut off and concealed under lacing of spruce root.

Pinock taking a break

Pinock taking a break, surprised by how much the filming slows the construction. This was the rarest moment for this hard worker. He was always impatiently watched by the camera crew who were concerned by the looming filming deadline.

Cedar ribs split

With the gunwales in place, it was back to splitting cedar into ribs for the canoe – about 1cm thick – and making endless amounts of even thinner 2–3mm sheeting.

Wood for splitting left to soak

Cedar splits best when it is damp so it is dutifully stored in the lake.

Undoing bundle of soaked wood

Thwarts carved and laced in

The thwarts for the canoe are made from black ash. These have to be split with wedges and carved down with the crooked knife. Having grown up working with ash wood this was an absolute joy to do.

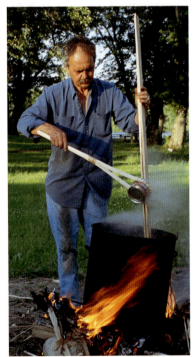

Ribs heated with hot water

The ribs are now heated with boiling water to soften them and make them pliable.

General view of canoe building

Without ribs to support it the bark hull sags like soft leather.

Ribs bent in pairs over knee

When pliable they are then bent in pairs over the knee.

Fitting ribs temporarily in place

As each pair of ribs is made they are forced down into the canoe and the gunwales are pulled upwards to stretch the bark taut.

Ribs set to shape deliberately oversized

Friction alone holds the ribs temporarily in place as they dry and take on the desired shape; they are left deliberately oversized so they can be trimmed once they have dried.

Ribs removed and trimmed to size

Now the ribs are marked, removed from the canoe and trimmed to their final size.

Fitting in ribs and sheeting

Between the ribs and the bark the sheeting is carefully placed – with the filming deadline looming we were forced to hurry this process. But no matter as this can easily be adjusted later on. The ribs are then fitted starting from the ends and working towards the centre. Considerable care and considerable force are employed to set them tight. They both give rigidity to the hull and stretch the bark taut.

Stem piece

The ends of the canoe obtain their strength from the stem pieces which are made by splitting a batten of cedar many times and heating it so that it bends like a laminate into the desired shape. This batten is then split lengthways into two identical pieces.

Stem pieces and little men

The stem pieces in turn are fixed with what are called the little men – boards on whose carved shoulders the gunwales rest.

The finished canoe

After all the joins in the bark had been sealed with melted spruce resin and bear fat, the canoe could be paddled. What a joy it was: as responsive as a feather, it soon earned the name *Goosefeather*.

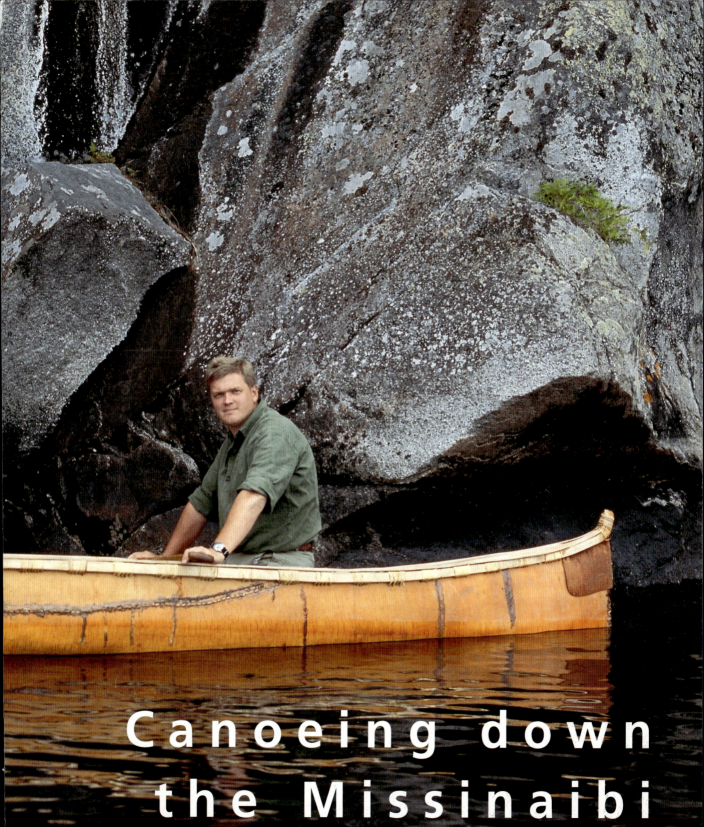

Canoeing down
the Missinaibi

Re-enacting a trader canoe in action: these boats were the superfreighters of their day, of enormous importance to the economy of Canada and beyond. Whatever you think of the fur trade, you have to marvel at the strength and speed of the voyagers. Their ghosts dwell on every waterway in Canada.

'What sets a canoeing expedition apart is that it purifies you more rapidly and inescapably than any other travel. Travel a thousand miles by train and you are a brute; pedal five hundred miles on a bicycle and you remain basically a bourgeois; paddle a hundred in a canoe and you are already a child of nature.'

The words of former Canadian Prime Minister Pierre Elliott Trudeau have always struck a special chord with me. As an outdoorsman I have always striven to experience nature in its purest form, and there is no better way of enjoying the wilderness than to glide down a river or lake on a canoe. You make no noise, you create no pollution, and you leave no more trace of your passing than the fading ripples and swirls from the tip of your paddle. If you want to feel at one with the natural world and observe the wildlife on shore undetected, travel by canoe.

The canoe was the first significant watercraft to be built by human beings and evidence of its existence in primeval times has been found all over the globe, but for me the spiritual home of the canoe will always be Canada. The canoe is central to Canadian culture because long before the introduction of railways and roads, the only way to penetrate the interior of the world's second largest country after Russia, was by its myriad of waterways. Even today, much of this vast wilderness remains accessible only by water, and although canoeing has become an almost exclusively recreational activity, it still provides a link to the country's past as well as access to some of the most beautiful and unspoiled environments on our planet.

(previous page) Lake Missinaibi, where the journey began, is a special place. The people who painted this rock art would have travelled here in birch-bark canoes just like this one.

A paddle that you have carved yourself has a life within
it that no factory-made model could ever possess.

Our journey began on the Missinaibi river in the province of Ontario, an historically important waterway that connects Lake Superior on the United States border with James Bay, which is roughly 500 km to the north east. It is an important route because Lake Superior was regarded as the gateway to the American West through which most traffic – human and commercial – passed before the introduction of the steam train in the second half of the nineteenth century. The river also played a key role in the early years of the fur trade when thousands of mainly French and British settlers took to the waters, braving severe conditions and natural obstacles in a quest to satisfy the enormous demand for animal pelts back in Europe and later on the eastern seaboard of North America.

The Missinaibi has remained largely uncorrupted by man's interference over the past four centuries and like all great rivers it demands to be treated with immense respect in all seasons. Man is never in charge on the Missinaibi. In springtime the river is a raging force, swelled and powered by the melting snow and ice of Canada's boreal winters, but in mid-summer its rapids remain a considerable challenge for even the most experienced of canoeists. By late summer the water level has dropped significantly but you still have to proceed with great caution, because the river's entire stretch is punctuated by rapids to tempt and test practised canoeists. But even the most arrogant paddler must pay homage at the great waterfalls where for but a brief few moments, the Missinaibi's gliding expanse narrows into thunderous cascades through steep, rocky outcrops – timely reminders of who is really the boss.

At these points you bow to its greater authority, leave the water and carry your canoe and equipment down trails known as 'portages'. The portage trails in many cases may be as old as the canoe itself, first established by the local Indians and then used by the trappers and voyageurs in the seventeenth and eighteenth centuries. You might think that the portage can be something of a slog as you head down an often steep, narrow path with a sixteen-foot canoe balanced on your head, especially towards the end of a hard day on the water with a swarm of mosquitoes trying to get at you. But in truth, excepting a few infamously long or swampy portage trails mostly these journeys are only a few hundred metres in length and make enjoyable breaks in the addictively hypnotic rhythm of paddling. To aid the carrying of my packs I employ an age-old tool of the north, the tumpline. This is a broad leather strap, which attaches to your packs and passes between the top of your forehead and the crown of your head. When first encountered these straps seem to be a torture device, but when you become accustomed to the subtlety of balance that they require, the tumpline becomes a powerful and comfortable ally, allowing you to carry several heavy packs at one go, reducing the number of times you walk the portage trail.

The birch-bark canoe can be carried by one man without great difficulty over the scores of portages strung along the banks of the rivers of eastern and central Canada. They are light and easy to manoeuvre with just a single paddle, but also very sturdy and capable of carrying heavy

loads. The European settlers were quick to recognise the qualities of their ancient Indian designs, adopting and adapting them for their own purposes. Today the various watercraft of the First Nation Canadians are still used as templates for the modern versions built with manufactured materials such as aluminium, plastic and fibreglass.

The original plan had been for me to paddle the traditional birch-bark canoe I had built with Pinock the week before but, sadly, large closely set lenticels in the bark caused concern over its strength, given the intention of running serious white water. The last thing we would have wanted was the canoe to break and provide the wrong impression. It is a sad reality that good birch bark is hard to find. In recent years the ravages of global warming and acid rain to say nothing of logging companies deliberately spraying birches with pesticides have all had their effect. Today birch bark tends to be thinner and more brittle than the thick rubbery bark found on canoes in museums. I have no doubt that the birch-bark canoes of yesteryear and those built today from the best bark can handle rapids as well as any other. In the event we did not want to risk the destruction of all our hard work, when one false move while running the rapids could shatter the craft into a thousand pieces of firewood. However, I did not like the idea of taking a plastic boat because I felt that it would have defeated part of the object of our journey, which was to show how traditional technology and design can be every bit as good as our modern equivalents. So I plumped for a traditional cedar canvas canoe – a Prospector design.

You may call me a romantic idealist if you wish, but in a way that I find difficult to justify and even harder to express I have always found a greater empathy for canoes made from natural materials. Wooden canoes need far greater care and maintenance than modern plastic boats, they are fragile where hydrocarbon hulls are resilient and they become heavier as they absorb water, where a modern boat shrugs off water from its petrochemical back. Despite all this a wooden canoe offers warmth to the touch like no other. When you paddle a cedar canvas canoe everything seems in accord with the river itself: even the sound of the water lapping against the canoe is right. When I paddle a Royalex plastic canoe, such is my devotion to this principle that the paddle must always be of wood, preferably hand carved. Such a paddle is rich with an imperfection and personality that imbue it with life in a way that no moulding ever can. Canoe and paddle are my interface with nature herself as in a votive way I offer myself up to the river.

Canoes like this made of cedar and canvas are used less often today but handle deep water and white water extremely well – they're a joy to paddle.

My challenge is to make the canoe dance in tune with the complex song of the river. At times this song is a gentle lullaby that reaches through the hull of the canoe to capture me totally in its spell – paddler, canoe, river, breeze, wildlife, united, undivided, one song, one being. At other times the tempo races as the river speeds me through rapids; if I am in tune with the river with an empty mind my paddle stroke and posture respond to the complexity of the puzzle that the river poses my bow. Joy comes with finding the 'line', that magic route of ease through a boiling sea of waves. But lose concentration for one moment and the spell is broken, and all grace goes out of the paddling as, buffeted by stopper wave and eddy line, I struggle for a while, perhaps sacrificing my intended route to paddle backwards through the tumult seeking a place of calm to pick up the tune again. Such is the magic of the canoe. But perhaps also in the back of my mind is the thought that when a wooden canoe is no longer repairable and it has spent its retirement alongside memories under the roof of an old man's shed, being all natural it will take one last voyage and return to the earth to nurture the growth of trees that perhaps will one day be fashioned into a new river craft to be called by that ancient Indian name, canoe.

Once we step down the route of traditional equipment a whole raft of other choices seem obvious. My equipment would be contained in traditional canvas and leather canoe packs. Originally designed for the purpose these traditional items stow perfectly into a canoe, they are practical, tidy and in keeping with the aesthetic. Inside these my gear will gain further protection from moisture by the judicious use of modern dry bags. For shelter I would be using a Baker tent. This traditional canvas tent gained popularity when used on film by the doyen of the Canadian canoe Bill Mason. A Canadian canoeing legend, artist, environmentalist, film maker and author, Mason favoured this style of tent as it provides a closeness with the natural environment while encouraging outdoor living rather than the temporary visitor atmosphere conjured in modern hike tents.

My companion for the journey would be an old friend, Ray Goodwin. Ray is one of Britain's leading canoeists. He would champion the more modern approach, using a Royalex 15-foot Mad River Explorer canoe, a carbon-fibre paddle, a plastic storage drum for his luggage and a synthetic, hi-tech tent.

Many decisions have to be taken when embarking on an expedition into remote areas, for example whether or not to take safety helmets. Clearly when training or play boating the use of a safety helmet is a prerequisite. But for us on this journey carrying a helmet would take up valuable space. After deliberation we chose not to

This was the view we had as we paddled – you can imagine how these great rivers became such important arteries for trade.

take them. Ray and I were of the opinion that if we needed to wear helmets then we should not be going to that remote location in the first place. It was a difficult decision to make because, with television cameras filming us throughout the week, we did not want to send out the wrong message to young or part-time canoeists. At the same time, we did not want to be slavishly beholden to the health and safety culture that has taken so much of the fun and adventure out of outdoor pursuits. We are both experienced canoeists and made a sensible, calculated judgement call that we were taking only a very small risk. Whenever we went through rapids, however, we did wear buoyancy aids. I tend not to wear a buoyancy aid on flat water unless the water is very cold or the weather is windy, but always wear one when running rapids. In short we did what we normally would do, without artifice for television.

With the history of canoeing filled with detailed descriptions of the great loads of furs and trade goods transported across North America's river systems, newcomers to canoe travel frequently paddle under the misconception that because the canoe is toting the load for you it is not important to travel light. This, though, is not the case; the importance of travelling light in wilderness cannot be overstated. Even the voyageurs were limited to forty pounds of personal equipment and clothing, a small allowance for the duration of the great voyages they were engaged in. Having said that lightness is an issue I can now temper the thought by saying that while travelling light we strive to live outdoors rather than just exist there. By this I mean that we carry the necessary equipment to travel in comfort for prolonged periods. For cooking we

'God grant me the serenity to walk the portage trails I must, the courage to run the rapids I can, and the wisdom to know the difference.'

can carry the tools and ingredients to make bannocks, cakes and pies, in fact a range of culinary delights less easily accomplished with the ultralight hiking cookset. Equipped with a small telescopic spinning rod and a good quality reel we can take advantage of our canoe to cast a 'Lucky Strike' 425 devil bait into a dark pool. This time-honoured red and white lure is still as productive as it ever was and has been sustaining northern canoeists since 1930. Not just a mere luxury, such culinary concerns are the very fuel of our journey for canoeing burns calories.

Waterproofing your kit and packing it well is the golden rule of canoe travel because we are constantly in the company of water and if it rains we are completely exposed in the uncovered craft. In the late summer when the water levels are relatively low, you may also encounter long stretches of rocky shallows. Then we must wade through the river, guiding the canoe with a length of rope in a process known as 'lining'. With the canoe lightened of the canoeist's weight, hopefully it can be steered through the shallows without scraping. Here the modern boat has an advantage, being far more tolerant of scraping against rocks than a canvas – or for that matter a birch-bark, hull. My colleague Ray could paddle dry-footed through stretches that I was forced to line, but no matter: I had the joy of watching this master paddler thread his way through the tangled ribbons of river, and the fun of paddling the challenging sections of white water. Even in the fur trade when the heavily laden voyageur boats had to pass by these ways there would have been one temptation every paddler knows and must come to respect: the temptation to run the rapid. The cargo carried by canoes of the past could only have made these decisions more critical. The risk of losing boat or cargo in rapids had to be balanced against the pressing need to transport the cargo as quickly as possible. There was no romance here: they needed to achieve forty paddle strokes a minute for eighteen hours a day when the rivers were unfrozen. The bourgeois and senior guides of the fur trade had to decide when to unload and portage the canoe and goods past the shallows, where to unload only the crew and track or line the rapid with ropes, where to move crew and load by the portage trail and line the boat 'demi charge' past the white water. Just as we must today, they had to decide when the rapid could be run and which line to take through the white water. Travelling as we were, in lightly loaded solo boats, we could paddle mostly where we wished and happily portage those falls that only angels can paddle. Bivouacked above split rock falls I watched as Ray Goodwin stood on the brink and looked down on the thundering river squeezing its way through the narrow canyon below. A man who has mastered every discipline of canoeing was searching for that golden line that perhaps in another type of boat he could use to run this rapid. He stood on the

In this environment you have to take great care with fire – this is on rock so it can't spread easily. Note the wanigan (old-fashioned larder box) and the wooden tripod and pot hook – the tools for making a nourishing hot meal.

brink not just of the canyon but of his very profession: taking their interest to the edge is what unites and drives inspirational outdoors professionals. Only gazing from such a vantage point can the dedicated pioneer see the possibility of a new way into the unknown, and a new place to know themselves. I watched with fascination and whispered the canoeists' prayer:

God grant me the serenity to walk the portage trails I must,
the courage to run the rapids I can,
and the wisdom to know the difference.

The Missinaibi and its banks are a timeless environment. Backed by tall poplars and spruce trees, majestic cedars sweep down to a river-side frill of Sagittaria leaves. There is barely any evidence of modern life to be seen, either on the river and its sprawling banks or in the vast expanses of woods that spread out to the distant horizons beyond. In places where logging activities have come close to the river, deep swathes of trees have been left on the river sides, effectively preserving the ambience and beauty of the river. The necessarily incongruent yellow plastic signs, which indicate the approach of a portage or waterfall, is all there is to distinguish this world from the one in which the hunters and trappers operated for over three hundred years from the early 1600s onwards. Those adventurous, pioneering Europeans may not have been there for the most noble reasons – in fact, they came close to wiping out Canada's huge beaver population which in turn would have wreaked havoc on the wilderness's delicately balanced eco-system – but you cannot fail to admire their courage and audacity as they took to canoes copied or bought from the local Indians to seek their fortune. Furs were a highly prized commodity and so great was the volume of trade in beaver that the skins became a currency or 'coin of the realm'. As late as 1820, for instance, a trapper could trade one beaver skin for one pound of shot, five pounds of sugar, half a pound of beads, a kettle, a pound of tobacco, two awls (for piercing holes), twelve buttons and twenty fish-hooks.

In the early days the trappers were mainly French, and their daring exploits as they headed into completely uncharted Indian-held territory have become the stuff of Canadian legend. In 1670 the English established the Hudson's Bay Company under a Royal charter granted by Charles II and although the company became the official face of the fur trade, there were, initially at least, many rival trappers working independently. Over the three centuries of its major fur-trading operation the company established dozens of trading stations along the shores of Hudson Bay,

James Bay, the Arctic Ocean and beyond into the western interior of this vast land. It's no exaggeration to say that the company provided the infrastructure upon which modern Canada has been built.

Each evening as we set up camp and settled down around our fire at the river's edge, you could not help but feel a powerful connection with those intrepid, hardy adventurers of the past. Today the campsites are marked, but little else has changed in the intervening years. Just as we were doing hundreds of years later, the voyageurs would have sat around the fire and cooked their food in a pot suspended from a tripod made from long branches. The sights, sounds and smells of the surroundings as they retired to spend the night under their overturned canoe would have been exactly the same. It is with good reason that the Canadians are extremely keen to preserve the pristine environment of their country's interior and they have imposed a raft of draconian laws to clamp down on the small minority of people who abuse their responsibility to look after the environment. In some wilderness areas of Canada, campfires are banned altogether and it is even illegal to carry bottles and cans on your journey. That seems a little severe at first, but we soon understood why the restrictions were there after coming across the odd pile of beer cans and other items of litter left behind by lazy visitors to the area.

For most people who enjoy the outdoor life, practising 'no trace camping' comes as second nature. All rubbish should be bagged and taken away when you leave. Nature will then operate its own cleaning-up process, flooding the riverbanks in the spring and washing away any evidence of human activity, such as the remains of your fire. In the Missinaibi area, you are advised to light your fire on rock, sand or gravel as the turf can smoulder for days and the fire can spring up somewhere else long after you have left.

It is easy today with the advantages of satellite phone communication and float planes to become complacent on a journey such as this. But it must be remembered that we are in a remote location which increases the level of risk associated with the rapids and requires a higher degree of self-reliance. The early travellers on these rivers, native and pioneering trappers alike, had one thing in common: they knew how to live with the land. They weren't just visitors, they brought their lives with them. They could take care of themselves, making and repairing their own equipment and when necessary feeding themselves from the land through their bushcraft. Today, few visitors to these waters have such knowledge, relying instead upon the food and other equipment brought along, as we were in many ways. Part of the reason for being there was to explore appropriate bushcraft and Ray Goodwin had asked me to help fill in the gaps in his rivercraft. A highly experienced paddler he had never had the opportunity to learn the skills that make life possible in the wilderness. I, of course, wished we had a whole year to really understand this environment, where seasonal moods are so powerful, but with only a short time available I decided on two fundamental skills necessary for the wilderness canoe paddler. The first of these was how to make an improvised paddle, because in a capsize it is all too easy to lose a paddle to the current. (For that reason we always carry a spare when paddling.) No canoeist wishes to be 'up the creek without one', so no bushcraft skill can be more fundamental to a canoeist than this. Like most things in bushcraft, this is a skill easy to comprehend from a book while you're sitting in an armchair, but which takes more skill than is apparent to put into action. Perhaps the single most important consideration is the choice of a suitable piece of wood. This is the task I set Ray, impressed that he had noticed standing dead cedar nearby. Cedar, while not as durable as other paddle woods – especially for white-water paddling – would be quickly and easily worked. Returning with a log of suitable dimensions (albeit with with grain not quite straight enough towards one end), we set to work. Using wooden wedges, called gluts, we split the log into two. With the axe, we flattened the curved side of the best half log to make a board. Using another paddle we marked out an ottertail-shaped blade, and with saw and axe cut out and further shaped the profile before finishing the blade with the crooked knife. It took half a day to make, good going when allowance for filming is made. Ray took the paddle out onto the water and, giggling with the joy that comes from a skill employed, he put it through its paces: 'Fantastic. From a log to a bow jam in a day.' (A bow jam is a natty way to turn a moving canoe which relies largely on a perfectly placed paddle.)

The next skill then must of course be fire-lighting. In the worst possible scenario

The forests are so dense here that the waterways have always been the only easy way through.

There's a routine to canoe travel. The days are long – you want to get as far as you can and it's better to be afloat than being bitten by mosquitoes on shore. In the evenings the fire is a place to relax and unwind. This Baker tent, as used by Bill Mason, creates a beautiful atmosphere not matched by other designs.

for a canoeist the canoe is lost – and perhaps with it all provisions and equipment. Fire in the wilds means life, dry warmth, safe water to drink, cheery light, signalling, cooking and so on and so forth. In wild country I never travel without a knife at the very least. With this tool and the appropriate knowledge it is possible to make just about anything else that you need.

For fire-lighting we employed the bow-drill method, ideal as the locally abundant cedar wood is one of the easiest materials to use for this purpose. With his knife Ray fashioned his equipment: the hearth board and drill from cedar, the top bearing block from another slightly harder wood. We made a bow from the bushes, took a piece of cord from the pocket of a buoyancy aid and we were in business. Without any fear of failure, Ray set about the task of producing an ember. After a couple of unsuccessful attempts he gradually modified his technique until, there in the notch cut into the hearth board, was a smoking ember ready and waiting to be placed in tinder and inspired into flame. More smiles as the flames rose in their smoke and his dependency upon shop-bought matches slipped away in the Missinaibi breeze. That night we discussed teaching and learning. Over the years we have both noticed a reluctance in many people to fail while learning and that those who care not about their appearance try more often, fail more often and seem to learn quicker. Perhaps in the dazzling lights of our media-dependent world we have lost sight of the many failures which must proceed success.

The Missinaibi may be one of the most pristine environments left on the planet but you still have to be careful about the water you drink. Viruses and bacteria, including Giardia, can be picked up from even the purest-seeming of waters, so it is sensible to use purifiers or boil your water. The local advice is that it is better to obtain drinking water from deep still pools, as Giardia is found on the surface of moving water. We used simple iodine-based water pumps, simply dangling the inlet pipe over the side of the canoe on slow stretches of the river and filling our canteens.

It takes a day or two to get back into the rhythm of canoeing and to shake the stiffness out of the muscles, but it was a wonderful feeling to set off each day onto the still surface of the river through the haze of the early morning mist. The magic of travelling by canoe is that you have to surrender yourself to the tempo of the river. You move at nature's pace, and the skill of canoeing is the way you angle the boat and use the paddle according to the currents, the breeze and the obstacles that lie in your way. It is only when you have had the experience yourself that you understand what canoeists mean by the thrill of the 'trinity' – man, boat and water – all working in unison. Sometimes the water is slow and you are the engine, paddling at a reasonable pace to drive you forward. At other times, the wind is blowing, the river is pulling beneath you and you simply trim and angle the boat accordingly to carry you along.

It is on the gentler stretches of the Missinaibi, of which there were plenty when we paddled it in the late summer, that you have the opportunity to observe the abundant life on and around the riverbanks. The beaver is now a common sight again in the Canadian wild having survived the savage depletion of its population at the hands of the trappers down the centuries. It is a shy, playful creature. But the area is also home to some predators, such as bear, cougar and wolves. We did not see any of these creatures on this particular journey, but we did wake up one morning to discover that some wolves had paid our campsite a visit in the night and chewed up some of our gear. There are a number of precautions you should take to minimise the chance of an unwelcome bear visit. Keep all food locked in airtight containers so that the bear is unable to pick up the scent and, before settling down for the night, hoist all provisions high into the branches using a long rope.

There are more than two hundred species of birds in the Missinaibi region as well as a great variety of fish including pike, walleye, sturgeon, bass and trout, but it was the sight of moose wallowing in the reedy waters close to the riverbank that gave us our most thrilling encounter with wildlife on this journey. This is when canoeing comes into its own. A canoe allows you to observe wildlife at extremely close quarters by approaching it with stealth and silence. There is a special paddling technique ideal for this, called the Indian Stroke, which involves manipulating the paddle with the fingertips and gently manoeuvring undetected through the water. Normally

Encounters like this are what canoe travel is all about – there is no other way
we would have got so close. Moose are the kings of the northern forest – and
he's got the crown to prove it!

you see a moose only from a distance but when you manage to get up close you realise what truly massive creatures they are. On this journey there were several occasions when we managed to get within a canoe-length of one.

The vast Canadian wilderness and the creatures that inhabit it are protected from degradation and destruction by strict environmental laws, but it has not always been that way. By the first half of the twentieth century, this was a world under growing threat from modern man's heavy-handed imposition on its delicate eco-system. However, thanks to the efforts of one of the century's most extraordinary and colourful characters, the wider world became aware of the threat to this magical environment and plans for its conservation were set in motion. His name was Grey Owl. Grey Owl was the epitome of the great adventurer, the first true eco-warrior, as well as a great writer whose books about the Canadian wilds were read by millions around the globe.

Grey Owl rose to prominence in the early 1930s preaching a gospel of conservation, before embarking on lecture tours around Great Britain and the United States, packing out arenas wherever he went and enthralling audiences with his beautiful evocations of the Canadian outback and his own simple life as an Indian. 'We need an enrichment other than material prosperity and to gain it we only have to look around to see what our country has to offer,' he wrote. The simple, natural way of life he described struck a particular chord with a generation ravaged by economic depression and standing on the brink of a second global conflict.

The day after his sudden death in 1938, not long after giving a personal address to King George VI and his two daughters at Buckingham Palace, the remarkable truth of his life and his real identity was revealed. Grey Owl was not, as he had claimed, the son of a Scotsman and an Apache mother, but was an Englishman from Hastings called Archie Belaney, who had sailed to Canada at the age of eighteen dreaming of being a Noble Indian. Within a few years Belaney was able to pass himself off as an indigenous Indian after growing out his hair, staining his skin and wearing authentic Indian dress. Without any intended malice he simply adopted the style of life which gave his troubled spirit the greatest comfort.

He emerged from the woods and resumed his original identity in order to serve in the Canadian Army in the First World War, but returned to his Indian guise and life at the end of the conflict – though not before he had married and deserted his childhood sweetheart while convalescing in

Grey Owl: 'My place is back in the woods, there is my home and there I stay.'

There are many places in this wilderness where access is only easy by float plane.

England. On his return from Europe, shattered by his experiences on the Western Front, he fell in love with a beautiful young Indian girl, a half-blood Mohawk called Anahareo. Disgusted by the cruelty of trapping animals to sell their fur, Anahareo told him that he had transgressed the Indian philosophy that he so espoused: for them all living things have a spirit and must be treated with respect. Surely a true Indian would only trap out of the need to find food? From that moment, until the day he died, Grey Owl committed himself to championing the cause of conservation.

Deprived of his income from trapping, Grey Owl agreed to become a living tourist attraction in a nature park, much to the amusement of the real Indians amongst whom he lived, who knew the truth about his origins. It was there in his little cabin – which he shared with a colony of beaver – that he began to write the books which brought him worldwide acclaim and fame. Thousands of tourists travelled to see him in the park.

When the truth about Archie Belaney was exposed, there was widespread shock and outrage throughout Britain, Canada and the United States. Those who had flocked to his lectures and had been transfixed by his hypnotic tales from the wilderness felt that they had been conned. But they had not, because when Grey Owl wrote of the wilds he wrote from detailed first-hand experience. He was not born an Indian and did not, as others in more recent years have, seek deliberately to falsify his upbringing to bring attention and riches upon himself. Instead when his enthusiasm for his cause reached a popular audience he rightly and unashamedly utilised this platform to pioneer the message that has become conservation. Even today this complex man of great contradictions remains an inspiration to many, in spite of all his flaws and fraudulence. You can only admire his spirit of adventure and his imaginative daring. But above all he should be applauded as the first true environmentalist of the twentieth century who, by the sheer power of his personal vision, helped to make the conservation of our natural surroundings one of the pressing issues of the world today. All credit to Canada too, for never abandoning him and cherishing the memory of the man who helped to save the beaver.

Not all the wildlife in Canada is so easy to admire and enjoy, and the greatest bugbear of our week on the Missinaibi was the swarm of mosquitoes that followed us on some days for long stretches of the river. For much of the summer mosquitoes are a nuisance on the river, but they were particularly bad during our visit in late June. (August is virtually free of all irritating insects and is probably the best time to go.) We protected ourselves as best as we could with repellents and netted headwear, but there was still no getting away from the mosquitoes and we often found ourselves being pursued downriver by clouds of them. You can go as fast as you like, but you will never out-paddle them.

The insects are no more than a minor inconvenience, however, and the real hazards of a canoe journey lie on the water itself. The Missinaibi is an extremely remote river and you have to take every precaution not to expose yourself or your companions to a serious accident. There is access to the river by float plane, but the number of places they can land is limited. Because the stakes are so much higher, you have to pay the river that much more respect and it would be unwise to take the risks that you might do in less remote locations.

That is one of the challenges I enjoy about truly wild places like Missinaibi. It is a real world, full of real dangers, and you cannot take to the rapids like a Hollywood stuntman. The priority is to look after the canoe because it is your greatest friend. Smash it on the rocks in a moment of recklessness and you will be stranded in the middle of nowhere without any equipment. In a plastic canoe you may be able to beat out the dents but the birch-bark and cedar canvas canoes will shatter on heavy impact with rocks and therefore they have to be handled with much greater dexterity. That presents an examination of skill that makes a journey so much more rewarding.

Our journey ended abruptly with a rendezvous with a float plane. I had to return to the UK where my father had been taken ill. All of a sudden the spell was broken as the float lifted off and my contact with the Missinaibi passed into memory. But as always with such trips, part of me will always be there and in a very real way the Missinaibi will always be a part of me.

On the
Trail of the
Mountain Men

When you arrive in Wyoming, it does not take long to understand why it is still known as 'The Cowboy State'. This vast land, the least populated state in the Union, is a throwback to a different age; a land of steepling mountain ranges, endless prairies, abundant wildlife, ancient Indian settlements and small, close-knit communities. Wyoming remains a true wilderness where you can sit around a campfire listening to old-timers tell you tales, passed down from their parents' generation, of Wild West legends such as Annie Oakley, Kit Carson, Buffalo Bill Cody and the great Jim Bridger, a personal hero of mine.

When you pack up your horse and head up into the mountains in Wyoming today, good bushcraft skills and knowledge are essential, just as they were for the frontiersmen of the nineteenth century. The only significant difference between then and now is that you can trek through this region in the confidence that you will not finish up on the end of an Indian arrowhead.

One of the reasons why the landscape is almost the same today as it has been for thousands of years is that there are fewer cars and roads in Wyoming than anywhere else in the United States. There is a great irony in that fact because it was here, along what was known as the Oregon Trail, that close to half a million migrants set out through an uncharted wilderness in search of a new life in California, Oregon and the other states of the American West. For a period of about twenty years in the mid-nineteenth century, this humble trail was the busiest thoroughfare in the States, with thousands of wagons strung out along its 2,000 miles from the Missouri river to the Columbia.

Now, as then, the trail amounts to no more than two scruffy wheel tracks barely visible in the prairie grass, but it is no exaggeration to describe it as one of the most important routes in American history. Part of the Oregon Trail was travelled by the famous frontiersmen Meriwether Lewis and William Clark in the early 1800s, and it was later used by the 'Mountain Men' and fur traders, but it was not until the 1840s that the great exodus of settlers from east to west began in earnest. Enticed by fanciful tales of an Arcadian paradise where wheat crops grew as tall as a man and root crops were five feet long, the European emigrants uprooted their families and risked their lives as they set off into the unknown.

The story of the Oregon Trail is both a great romance and a stirring epic, but it is the tales of Jim Bridger and the other Mountain Men who preceded the settlers that holds the greatest fascination for me. Jim Bridger was a superb woodsman, an expert trapper and guide, a true pioneer, who played a major role in opening up the west of the United States. He was probably the best known of the Mountain Men, a hardy group of hunters and traders of whom there were never more than about five hundred in total but whose exploits have become part of American folklore. These men mingled with the friendly Indians, quickly learning their skills in order to survive in an

The Oregon Trail is still clearly visible today.

extremely harsh and dangerous environment, and even adopting many of their manners, beliefs and dress. Earning up to $2,000 in a season, the rewards were high for Bridger and his fellow fur traders, but the risks were even greater.

Jim Bridger was an unusual Mountain Man in that he died of old age. Most of them died on the point of an arrow or spear of a hostile Indian, but there were plenty of other potentially fatal hazards too. Rattlesnake bites, attacks by grizzly bears, climbing accidents, diseases such as dysentery and smallpox, and drowning in the raging rivers also accounted for scores of these bold frontiersmen. Bridger, who was twice married to Indian women, was reputed to have been the most daring and courageous of them all and he once had to have the arrowhead of a Blackfoot Indian cut out of his back – but not until he had completed his mission up in the mountains several weeks later.

When I visited Wyoming I wanted to experience its magnificent wilderness just as the Mountain Men had done. This, as it quickly transpired, was not going to be very difficult to arrange because, to this day, travelling as Bridger and his companions had done remains the *only* way to experience it. There are no roads, no shops and no hotels. The only way to get about is on horseback, the only place to sleep is in a tent, or in the open if it is warm enough, and the only thing to eat is what you take with you or what nature can offer. Local knowledge is essential in this environment and we were fortunate to be accompanied by a local guide called Tory Taylor, an expert horse packer, ecologist and gifted amateur archaeologist.

The beauty of the landscape is as breathtaking as anything I have ever seen, but it is a treacherous place too, even for the most experienced trekkers, and it can be difficult to traverse even on horseback. Travelling by horse really gives you a powerful sense of what it must have been like for the Mountain Men, but you can only imagine the awe they must have felt when they first laid eyes on the land formation known as the Continental Divide. The drainage from Wyoming's huge mountain ranges, which are covered in snow and ice for nine months of the year, runs into four main headwaters: the Colorado, Columbia and Missouri rivers and the Great Salt Lake. All the water on one side of the divide eventually runs into the Atlantic Ocean and on the other into the Pacific.

As we stopped to take in the panorama before us, it was difficult to take on board that until just a few generations ago this region was the western frontier of the United States, and it was only in 1890 that Wyoming became the forty-fourth state of the Union. Much of the terrain remains almost impassable today, in spite of the numerous expeditions sent out by the federal government to try to find a way to get across the divide.

Leo Lajeunesse is a Shoshone whose great grandfather was Jim Bridger's guide. He is also related to Minnie Boyd, close friend of the legendary Butch Cassidy.

With its arid desert, short-grass prairie and alpine climates there is an enormous diversity of landscape to experience in Wyoming, but the weather there is hugely unpredictable too. You can be basking in glorious sunshine under clear blue skies in the morning and battling through three feet of snow in the afternoon. An average of 200 inches of snow fall on the mountains of Wyoming each year and temperatures in January are an average of minus 12 degrees centigrade. This, in short, is not country for the faint-hearted or the ill-prepared.

The Mountain Men who lived out here for months on end had to be quick learners, especially in the winter months, and only the hardiest and most resourceful survived. Other than flour, coffee and tea, these frontiersmen carried no provisions with them, and they had to rely on their bushcraft and hunting skills for their sustenance. The Mountain Men would kill any animals they could find, including buffalo, deer, elk, antelope, rabbit – even wild cat and wolf – but they would also eat nuts, wild fruits and roots.

One of the most striking features about this area is the wildlife which is almost as abundant today as it was then. Deer, bear, elk, pronghorn, moose, bison, beaver, wolf, rabbit, quail, partridge, grouse, pheasant and wild turkey are all found here. Some species, like the bison and wolf, faced extinction but thanks to man's more beneficial interference in recent times, their numbers are growing again. I have always felt that man has a responsibility to help redress the natural balance of environments and habitats that he has spent so many centuries upsetting.

The animal kingdom featured in almost every area of the daily lives of the Mountain Men. Like the Indians they lived alongside, they relied on animals for their survival, hunting them too for their skins and hides which they either used for their own purposes or traded on their return from the wilds. Horses were of crucial importance and the Mountain Men took great care to ensure they were well looked after. Without horses to carry you and your kit through this rugged region, the going soon gets extremely tough. Horses were also highly coveted by local Indians, who were eager to capture them from the white man and thereby raise their standing within their community. The two most important possessions to a frontiersman in these parts were his horse and his hair. To lose your horse was almost as disastrous as being scalped.

Just as the frontiersmen had done 150 years earlier, we also recognised that the relationship between man and horse is a partnership. Each day when we

A successful partnership between man and horse has always been important
here: looking after them properly is crucial to survival in this terrain.

set up camp for the night, our first priority was always to attend to our horses, which we would put out to graze after untacking them and removing all our equipment from their backs. They had looked after us all day, now it was our turn. The horses have to be 'hobbled' by chaining their front legs together, which gives them the freedom to graze freely, but stops them from running away.

It is also important to hang bells around their necks as a deterrent against the black bears and grizzlies that still roam this remote territory. It is estimated that there were roughly 100,000 grizzly bears in North America in the nineteenth century, but relentless hunting brought them close to extinction, and today they are a fairly rare sight. Estimates suggest that there are now fewer than 1,000 grizzlies in the United States, but we saw plenty of evidence of their presence during our trek and you still have to be on your guard when sleeping out in the open as we were. Tell-tale signs that bears were at large were the several trees we came across which had been stripped of their bark. We also saw some fresh bear tracks on our trail suggesting that a mother and a cub had recently passed that way.

The paw print of a young grizzly bear

When camping in these parts you must be careful about bears stealing your food: note the special bear-proof metal storage container.

I have never had a problem with grizzlies and I have managed to get to within a few feet of these giant, intelligent beasts in the past. But you have to respect the bear at all times, and especially so when they have young cubs in train. Bears can kill people or other animals with a single blow of a mighty paw. Fully grown grizzly bears can weigh up to a staggering 1,500 pounds and can reach speeds of up to 35 mph. They feed on a variety of plants, berries, roots, fish and small mammals, but they are scavengers too and will help themselves to anything humans might have been foolish enough to have left about their campsite. Many people think that the bears are the problem but in fact it is us, the humans who unwittingly invite bears into our campsites by not taking the proper precautions with our provisions. It is usually hunters who have the biggest problem because bears want to disinherit them of their kill. In the Greater Yellowstone Ecosystem, a vast tract of land straddling the states of Wyoming, Montana and Idaho and incorporating the famous national park of the same name, it has been made compulsory for visitors to store their food in a secure metal container known as a bear box, or to hang it from a container high up in the trees.

195

Buffalo, awesome creatures whose fur and meat have been so important to the way of life here for thousands of years.

Jake Korell, mountain man.

When setting up camp in this wilderness, you have to be alert to its dangers at all times, but in the warmer months I still prefer to camp out under a tarp rather than in a tent because you feel that much closer to nature. Jim Bridger felt the same way and when he was living out for months on end he used to curl up on the ground with just a buffalo robe for warmth and comfort. It is said that he hated going to town because he found hotel beds too soft and used to sleep on the floor instead.

Sitting around a campfire and listening to the tales of the locals is one of the great joys of travelling in this region, and I like to get a fire going as soon as possible once we have managed to get the rest of our site in good order. Pine knots, of which there are plenty to be found in Yellowstone, are an excellent source of fuel and you do not need too many of them to create a very hot, bright fire that will last long into the night. Less fuel means less work too, and snapping off a couple of armfuls of these small knotty pine branches from fallen trees means you do not have to waste a great deal of valuable daylight chopping and collecting logs.

While we were in Wyoming we spent some time with a modern-day equivalent of Jim Bridger by the name of Jake Korell, a colourful ninety-year-old who has been trapping beaver since he was seven. The way Jake catches beaver is broadly similar to how the hunters would have gone about it almost two centuries ago, although today the traps are considerably more humane. Back in the early nineteenth century, the hunters baited the traps with some greenery, twigs and a substance called castoreum which is extracted from the beaver's musk glands. The traps were then placed under the surface of the water and the beaver drowned when it got caught. Jake showed us how to skin the animal and stretched the hide over a round metal frame for it to dry. Today the money to be made from beaver skins is a fraction, in real terms, of what Jim Bridger and his companions would have received for their efforts and Jake told us he would be paid no more than about $25 (around £15) for a skin. Profit is no longer the motivation for trapping, and it is simply a case of keeping the beaver numbers down to a reasonable level in order to maintain the right natural balance for the delicate eco-system of the area. A beaver can quickly transform a farmer's paddock or field into a lake by damming a nearby stretch of river.

After trapping and skinning the animal, Jake prepared a delicious stew with its meat, and as we sat around the campfire eating it and listening to his tales about Jim Bridger, Annie Oakley and other Wild West characters, we were reminded of how little has changed in this wild corner of the world since the early settlers began to roll across the Oregon Trail all those years ago. It was strange but thrilling to reflect that Jake had grown up with people who had been friends with the great cowboy characters and frontiersmen whose legendary exploits have enchanted generations of

Jake Korell shows how, having trapped a beaver, he removes the skin before stretching it on a circular frame to dry.

people around the globe. When you talk to a character like Jake, you realise quite how recently the great adventures of the Wild West took place.

The following morning we were treated to an extraordinary spectacle. As I looked out across the valley I saw some movement in the prairie grass about 600 feet from our camp and on closer inspection realised it was a pack of wolves feeding on a kill. Once this would have been a fairly common sight but today it is extremely rare, and we had been told that it was highly unlikely that we would get to within a mile or two of any. The wolf, one of my favourite animals, has suffered as much as any wild creature in these parts over the past two centuries and they were only reintroduced to the region as recently as 1995. Incredibly, this was the first occasion that our guide Tory had ever seen one of these elusive beasts in this area. You can count such encounters with the wolf on one hand and we were aware of how privileged we were.

We followed the pack's tracks into the woods as far as we could before we headed our own way. As we journeyed deeper into the mountains, we encountered some truly tough terrain to traverse, even on horseback. The paths are treacherously narrow and steep on some stretches and they are often flanked by dense forest, which would have provided perfect cover for ambushes by hostile Indians in Bridger's day. In an area like this, with its endless forests and bewildering range of rocky peaks and hidden valleys, it is extremely easy to get lost and it is essential that you know where you are at all times. Bridger famously once said of his travels through the Wyoming mountains: 'Often I didn't know where I was for two or three days but I was never lost.'

One man who did get lost but managed to find his way out of this vast, inhospitable wilderness was a character called Hugh Glass, who was, if you like, the Mountain Man's Mountain Man. Glass, who was of Irish stock and was said to have been a pirate before settling in the American West, was badly mauled by a bear on a hunting expedition with Bridger in the summer of 1823. Glass was out scouting the terrain with some other members of the expedition when he found himself caught between a female grizzly bear and her two cubs. With one ferocious swipe the mother grizzly slashed Glass's body from head to foot. His fellow hunters carried him on a litter for several days but his wounds were dreadful and it was considered to be just a matter of time before he passed away.

The party were travelling through hostile Indian country and, not wanting to risk the entire party for one man, it was decided that Bridger and another man called John Fitzgerald would stay with Glass while the rest continued their trek. After several days of waiting for Glass to regain consciousness, Bridger became convinced

Lake Washakie is a reservoir formed by flooding an ancient Shoshone camping ground. Wyoming is rugged yet stunningly beautiful: for the Native Americans it was their birthright, for the European settlers it was a land of promise and opportunity.

This land has a bloody history: the vivid colours of a Shoshone cemetery with its monuments to eminent Shoshone and the stark message of a plaque marking the death of two white settlers.

that there was no hope of him recovering from his wounds and they decided to abandon him, taking his gun with them, but leaving the basic equipment to help him survive if he did ever regain consciousness. When the pair emerged from the mountains, they reported to the other hunters that Glass had died of his injuries. In the meantime, however, Glass had come round and, desperately weak from his injuries and lack of food, he set off on all fours to try to find his way out of the mountains. As he crawled through the woods and along riverbanks he ate wild berries, roots and the flesh of dead animals to sustain him, but he knew he would die unless he treated the infection which had developed in the deep wounds inflicted by the bear. The legend goes that his solution to the problem was to lie down on a rotting log and let the maggots eat the infection out of his back.

Slowly he regained some of his strength and in the final stages of his remarkable journey he was able to stand and walk upright and, with the help of some friendly Indians, he eventually reached Fort Kiowa where his appearance like some ghost from the past, together with the story of his survival, caused astonishment. News of his escape from the wild spread like bushfire throughout the West and word got out that Glass was so furious with Bridger and Fitzgerald for taking his gun that he set out to find them and reclaim it. At one point on his journey through the wilderness he took a boat on the river, but it was moving so slowly that he asked to be put ashore so that he could walk instead, even though it meant covering a far greater distance. Shortly after he disembarked, the boat was attacked by Indians and everyone on board was killed. It is difficult to separate fact from fiction in Glass's adventure, but it is said that when he finally tracked down Fitzgerald, he walked up to him and said, 'Give me back my gun,' and Fitzgerald duly obliged.

Today, little remains of the once great native civilisations of North America. Of all the ancient peoples of the world we visited in the course of filming our television series, it was the Indian communities of the United States whose traditional way of life had been the most severely compromised by the influence and encroachment of the modern world. We headed to an Indian Reservation known as Wind River to see what remained of the Shoshone culture. The belongings of these nomadic people were made of natural, degradable materials and have long since been returned to the earth. A circle of flat stones embedded in the ground on the site of an abandoned Indian encampment was the only lasting monument of Indian culture that we came across in the area. You could only imagine what it must have been like when the site was home to a thriving,

These Choke cherries have always been an important food source here: rich in Vitamin C, once gathered they are crushed before being dried over an open fire on a simple framework of branches.

eft, our camp at Wind River

ancient community with dozens of buffalo-hide tipis, smoking fires and a field of horses.

The early settlers and hunters used Indian sign language to converse with the Shoshone, who were friendly to the white settlers. Even though he was illiterate, Jim Bridger understood the value of being able to communicate with the Indian tribes and he became fluent in sign language as well as Shoshone and other dialects. Nowadays everyone converses in English, providing further evidence of a culture that has seen much of its proud tradition trampled underfoot by the galloping pace of modernisation. There was one character there who had learned many of his skills and crafts by reading books written by white men, and we witnessed him being put in his place by one of the community's spiritual elders. 'You have given yourself an English name, but what is it in your own language?' the elder asked. When the man couldn't answer him, the elder laughed and walked away.

While the natural environment in which the Indians lived remains largely unchanged, much of their traditional way of life has either disappeared, taking with it a whole raft of ancient bushcraft skills, or it is kept secret from outsiders. We got a very powerful feeling throughout our visit there that the Shoshone people had been exploited so much and so often down the years that they had decided, consciously or otherwise, that they were no longer willing to share their knowledge and customs with others, no matter how respectful and friendly they might be. But there could be no doubting their deep attachment to their heritage and ancestors, and when they took us to their cemetery we were all deeply moved by the experience. Whereas in our graveyards you might see the odd wreath or bunch of flowers on a tombstone, this Shoshone cemetery was alive with colour in an atmosphere of profound reverence.

As nomads it was important for the Indian tribes to

Constructing a bull boat: first you hammer in four stakes, using the buffalo hide as a guide to make sure the frame will be the correct size. Then the willow stems are woven to provide the frame before the hide is attached using strong buffalo skin sinews.

prepare food that could be stored for a long period of time. Pine nuts, pemmican and jerky were all staples of the Indian diet while the multitude of waterways were another obvious source of food. We were shown the simple but ingenious way the Indians used to catch fish. After wedging funnel-shaped wooden traps between the rocks, the Indians scared the fish from their resting places and forced them into the traps further downstream. The fish were then carried back to the encampment where they were filleted and dried on racks over fires to create a long-lasting staple food to take on the trail.

In order to travel through this area or to transport goods without having to divert miles from their intended path the Indians, and the Mountain Men who followed them, had to be able to cross a myriad of lakes, rivers and tributaries. They did this in a very simple craft, similar to the coracle, known as a bull boat, which can be built in a day and is capable of carrying loads of up to half a ton despite weighing only about thirty pounds. The framework of the bull boat is made of willow branches which are bent into shape and then lashed to a dried buffalo hide with the hair side facing outwards to create a watertight covering.

Jim Bridger once accepted a bet that he could not navigate the Bear River and duly set off in a bull boat he had built himself. After negotiating the river for hundreds of miles he found himself in a vast expanse of water. The story goes that Bridger felt that the boat was far more buoyant than it had been in the river and so he tasted the water – and it was salty. When he finally returned to the mountains to claim his winnings from the bet and told his companions about his experience, they were convinced he had reached the Pacific Ocean. In fact, he had discovered the Great Salt Lake.

For me, that story sums up the magic of this region and the pioneering age in which Bridger lived. It was a period of great discoveries and adventures in which a small group of men with a profound knowledge of bushcraft pushed into unknown territory to open a new world for future generations. But the opening of the trail to the fabled lands of the American West was finally achieved thanks not just to the daring of those Mountain Men, but also to the ancient skills of the Native Americans. The tragedy of the story is that those skills, and the great Indian cultures from which they sprang, were all but lost in the process.

The stones of a ruined eagle trap: the Shoshone would build a small hut roofed with branches. Meat was put on the roof as bait, then a Shoshone would hide in the 'hut'. When an eagle landed, the Shoshone would reach up and seize as many of the prized eagle tail feathers as he could.

Sweden,
Land of Living
Bushcraft

Winter arrives gradually in Northern Sweden, as frost seeps into the landscape. Then comes the snow, cloaking the land in an icy blanket which lasts for nine months of the year.

Temperatures can drop as low as minus 40 degrees centigrade. In the very depths of winter the sun never rises, and for the rest of the time its daily appearance is pitifully brief. The landscapes of northern Scandinavia are beautiful in their bleakness, but they were not designed for human habitation. For centuries, though, the nomadic Sami people somehow managed to make this frozen wasteland inside the Arctic Circle their home.

In order to survive in one of the coldest, harshest environments on the planet, those remarkable inhabitants had to develop a deep knowledge of bushcraft, but the traditional lifestyle of the Sami has disintegrated significantly over the past two or three decades. Where once they roamed the wind-blasted tundra protected from the elements by nothing more than a tipi-style tent made from reindeer skins, nowadays they live in solid houses. Those who do follow the reindeer today do so on snowmobiles rather than skis, but they do still use the traditional shelters. Only a generation ago, tens of thousands of Sami subsisted entirely on the reindeer herds which they followed around the land according to the animals' migration patterns, but today most of them hold jobs in the mainstream economy. However, in spite of the great changes that have swept through their society like an Arctic blizzard, much of the Sami culture and many of their survival skills have endured. Old customs thaw slowly for these hardy people, and their powerful bond with the land and the wildlife that sustained them for so long is preserved and celebrated in song, religious custom, art and crafts, and an ongoing struggle for political recognition.

But it is not only the Sami who enjoy a special relationship with their natural environment in Sweden. Whereas most Britons live in sprawling conurbations and have lost that ancient intimacy with their surroundings, in Sweden 'the nature', as it is called, remains an integral part of the wider culture. In a land of such size and beauty there is simply no getting away from it. At school young Swedes are taught the arts of orienteering, while the sacrilege of dropping litter is drummed into them from the earliest age. Throughout Sweden there is recognition that the traditional skills of bushcraft are something to be cherished, not as a historical curiosity, but as a valuable and enriching part of people's lives. Engineering – bushcraft's industrial cousin – is a prestige job in Sweden, whereas in Britain these days it is an occupation without glamour or great respect.

Sweden is a country with an abundance of natural resources – more than 60 per cent of it is covered by forest and there are more than one hundred

thousand lakes scattered across the landscape. Many of those lakes are so clean you can drink the water from them without having to boil or purify it first. In Britain 'the right to roam' has only recently been enshrined in law but the inhabitants of Sweden have enjoyed what they regard as their birthright since medieval times. Literally translated, 'allemansratten' means 'every man's right' and the ancient custom grants citizens and tourists alike the entitlement to enjoy the natural surroundings without undue restriction of access. People are allowed to cross another man's land and to remain there for a short period, with the strict proviso that they do not abuse that privilege in any way.

Sweden is an outdoorsman's paradise and I have made many visits there over the years. I still find it incredible that just a few hours after boarding an airplane in England I can be trekking through the snows of a Swedish forest, collecting pinewood for a fire or cooking up some fish, freshly caught from beneath the thick ice of the lake's surface. Sweden is a country where the seasons are equally enchanting and I particularly enjoy going there in the autumn when the landscape has yet to be transformed into a frozen paradise. It is no exaggeration to say that canoeing and camping in Sweden at that time of year is the closest I have come to a religious experience.

There is a magnificent stillness about the surroundings and, with barely a ripple on the water's surface, you can sit by your fire at the water's edge, listening to woodpeckers hammering for their food in the bark of a tree over a mile away. The final wild berries of the season still hang from the trees and bushes, but you can feel winter fast approaching as the days shorten and you have to be productive with the time that daylight grants you. One of the most commonly eaten wild fruits in Sweden is the lingonberry, also known as the cowberry. The lingonberry is an excellent natural preservative and it is also eaten with meat dishes in the same way that we use cranberries and redcurrants with our Sunday lunch back home.

On my last visit to Sweden I met up with my old friend Lars Falt, a Swedish survival expert, who brought with him an Arctic charr as a gift for our supper. Lars's present, however, came with a condition: namely, that I had to cook this delicious fish with its vibrant orange-red flesh, in the traditional Alaskan way. The way to do this is to ease the ribs away from the

My old friend Lars Falt, companion on many an expedition in these parts, watches over the Arctic charr which I'd panissed – a excellent way to cook fish over an open fire.

The panissed charr with lingon-berries, cooked and ready to eat.

meat using the thumbs, keeping all the bones and fins for a stock so that nothing is wasted. Then you insert two or three sticks crossways through the fish to hold it open before lashing it all to a longer stick, which is then stuck into the ground at an angle so that it is the right distance above the fire. When it is ready, I recommend sprinkling it with lingonberries to give it an extra blast of flavour. As an accompaniment I used a large brown mushroom from the sarcodon family of which there are dozens of different species, but I like to call this particular variety the 'deerhair' fungus owing to the fine texture of its underside.

The Swedes have always made good use of one of their greatest natural resources – the pine tree. The pungent tar extracted from the tree was known as 'the black gold of Sweden' and for centuries small landholders in the north produced it as a cash crop, exporting barrels of it abroad, much of it to Britain where boat-builders used it as a preservative coating for a ship's wood and rigging. It is no exaggeration to say that the Royal Navy was kept afloat by this remarkable natural product for many years. Until European settlers began to open up the forests of North America in the eighteenth and nineteenth centuries Sweden was the world's biggest producer of pine tar. The Swedes made use of the tar for medicinal purposes too, mainly as an antiseptic, but it is also an effective mosquito repellent. Today pine tar is still used by tree surgeons for healing trees and shrubs which have been damaged in some way, while it can also be used for treating animal hooves, as well as cuts to sheep and cattle.

We saw the process of extracting tar ourselves when we visited a character called Ake Carlsson who has spent an entire working life producing the 'black gold'. The methods have changed a little down the years, but the principles have remained the same. The roots of the pine tree contain such a great concentration of tar that it is possible to light them with a match, and when you hold them the lovely stench of turpentine is overwhelming. Ake knows exactly where to look for the roots of old trees and the clump he lifted from the ground for us could have been hundreds of years old. After breaking up the roots Ake placed them into a metal vat before lighting them and sealing the lid. When the temperature reaches 430 degrees centigrade the tar begins to seep from the roots in considerable quantities.

Ake Carlsson shows us how to produce 'black gold': pine roots are burned in a vat until the tar runs out.

Bjorn and I felled a pine tree from which he was able to cut, shape and bend two beautiful wooden skis, before coating them with the 'black gold'.

In the old days of mass production the tar would have been collected in a long trench beneath the fires, but today Ake uses a pipe connected to a container. Those trenches used to collect up to five thousand litres of the tar, and it was amazing to see quite how much of the fluid our small pot of roots produced.

One of the many uses to which the Swedes put the tar was in the making of skis. Before the invention of the snow mobile people in Sweden had to rely on their skis to move around the countryside in the winter. Today skis are mass-manufactured from metal but for centuries they were made of wood – usually from birch or pine – and the craft of making wooden skis is still practised today. The oldest ski in the world was found in a swamp in Sweden and dates back more than five thousand years, but the method of its construction would not have been significantly different from the techniques used in far more recent times.

It was fascinating to watch local craftsman Bjorn Jonsson make a pair of skis in the traditional manner, using only natural materials and starting with nothing but an axe and a saw to chop down the pine tree from which they were to be fashioned. The best type of tree to use is one that is dead – but not rotten – because the wood is drier. The humble pine is a truly remarkable tree and its wood is soft yet durable and excellent for carving. Bjorn and I chopped down a tree using a two-man saw; first you have to chop out an apex with an axe, then saw just above it from the other side so that the tree falls away from you.

After splitting the trunk into four lengths, using wooden wedges to prise the wood apart, Bjorn sawed them into planks before he set about shaping them, using the traditional 'axing' method. In order to soften the wood, Bjorn steamed them over a pot of boiling water before bending the front of the skis into an upward curve that makes it easier to travel through deep snow. The skis were then placed into a type of clamp overnight and fastened with birch bindings in order to secure their shape, after which they were coated with pine tar to preserve and protect them. The finished skis were not just objects of great beauty and examples of superb craftsmanship, they were also highly efficient, good quality pieces of equipment. 'To set out on skis you have made yourself is a great experience,' Bjorn told us.

Pinewood makes an excellent charcoal as it lights very easily and burns very hot. We witnessed its qualities for ourselves when we visited a Swedish blacksmith, Julius Pettersson, who crafted a knife blade for me using exactly

Another fine craftsman: Julius Pettersson works at the anvil in his forge.

Julius works the red-hot metal for the
knife before grinding the edge.

the same techniques and skills employed by his ancestors for centuries before him. The knife holds a special place in Swedish culture, where it is still very much regarded as a tool, not a weapon. I remember when I first started going to Sweden and I was a little taken aback to see men walking around the airport with knife sheaths in their belts. The knife has been demonised in modern British culture, but in Sweden it remains an essential tool for anyone working or living outdoors. It is put to a myriad of different uses out in the wild, and if a man falls through thin ice it could make the difference between life and death as he struggles to get out of the icy water as quickly as possible.

The economy of effort with which Julius performed what is a highly skilled task was wonderful to behold. He made it look so easy as he folded the red-hot iron around a high carbon steel core before hammering the blade into shape, and forming the tang to be inserted into the handle. After grinding the blade to give it its edge he then quenched it in warm oil to harden it and make sure it was non-magnetic. He then heated it again, more gently this time, in order to draw out some of the hardness and make it less brittle. When you feel the finished article of a handmade blade like this one, you realise that it has a life and energy that a mass-produced, stainless steel equivalent can never match.

I took the blade with me when we headed north into the Sami heartlands where there are still hundreds of craftsmen producing ornate carved handles in the traditional style. Today the Sami craftsmen produce their goods for the tourist industry, but it was heartening to know that the ancient bushcraft skills of their forefathers are still being put to a useful end. For me, a large part of bushcraft is about combining modern and ancient expertise, and the Sami have become masters of that practical philosophy.

The Sami, also known as Lapps, have lived and roamed in northern Scandinavia, across Norway, Finland, Russia and Sweden, for thousands of years. They followed the movements of their reindeer herds across swollen rivers and frozen tundra, from mountain to valley, depending on the season – of which there are eight in the Sami calendar. The whole family would follow the herds, living in turf huts or tents known as 'lavvus' which are made from reindeer skins and simple wooden poles and have a hole in the top to let out the smoke from the fire around which they congregated in the dark days of winter. The arrival of settlers in southern Scandinavia led to the Sami being pushed further and further into the bitterly inhospitable north. Reindeer formed the staple of their diet for most of the year, but in the summer they supplemented it by hunting, fishing and an abundance of wild berries.

It is estimated that there are about sixty thousand Sami today, but times have

These huts, called Torv Kata, are perfectly designed to keep out the intense cold with roofs of turf acting as excellent natural insulation.

Per-Nils, a typical modern Sami

changed and they no longer live as nomads. Nor do the majority of the Sami rely on reindeer to make a living any more; instead they now work as fishermen – both coastal and freshwater – as well as farmers, foresters and miners, while many others have migrated to cities and towns in search of employment. Most Samis, however, still have at least one relative involved in reindeer farming and although traditional herding practices have been replaced by snowmobiles, helicopters and boats, the reindeer remains fundamental to Sami culture. It is sometimes said that if you put a Sami in a room full of people he feels dizzy, disorientated and does not give a great account of himself, but take him outside and send him off into the teeth of a biting wind, back into his natural element in other words, then he feels at home once again.

During our stay in northern Sweden we were introduced to a character called Per-Nils, who still makes a living from herding reindeer. Per-Nils lives a physically demanding, dangerous life, especially in the autumn and spring months when the snow is not hard. In his world a man has to be entirely self-reliant – for the simple reason that he has no choice but to be. He spends days at a time out in the wilderness by himself and there is no one there to help him if finds himself in danger.

Per-Nils is the embodiment of the practical Sami, combining new equipment and practices with the old ways. For him, it is all a question of whatever works the most efficiently, and it was interesting to note what he was wearing. A modern Gore-Tex jacket, he explained, offered him greater flexibility and ease of movement as well as a good number of pockets, but like many of the Sami he spurns the use of modern-style boots and trousers because their traditional equivalents, made from reindeer skin, are tougher, warmer and longer lasting. Before giving us a demonstration in the ancient Sami skill of lassoing reindeer, Per-Nils also showed us how he preferred to stuff his boots with grass – the carex species of sedge – rather than use socks. He uses the sedge not out of any blind sentimentality for a long-held tradition, but because it is warmer and dries more quickly than socks. Per-Nils' skills mock the arrogance of many of those who take to the outdoors today equipped with all the modern gizmos and gadgetry, but with none of the spirit and wisdom of real bushcraft based on a true understanding of nature.

It is almost impossible to overstate the importance of the reindeer to their traditional culture and even today, for Sami earning their livings in other ways, the animal retains a mythical hold on them. Without the reindeer, the Sami could never have survived. They owe their very existence to them. It used to happen occasionally that a family's entire herd of several hundred reindeer would perish when panic broke out while making a perilous river crossing in springtime. In a few chaotic moments, the fragile existence of that family would come to an end.

Every single part of the reindeer was put to some use: its flesh, organs and milk for eating, its skin for clothing and equipment, its antlers for carving into knife handles and other tools, its sinews for general sewing purposes and tying up the lavvu.

Using traditional Sami methods I made a handle for the blade that Julius had fashioned for me down south. After cutting some rough pieces of antler for the ends, a small block of wood for the middle and a few strips of leather to go in between them, I slotted them into the right order and then glued them together before getting down to the laborious but highly satisfying task of filing the handle into the desired shape.

Per-Nils' wife, Brit-Marie, is an expert carver and the ornate intricacy of the patterns on her knife handles is breathtaking. After cutting out hundreds of minuscule grooves she makes a powder from the inner bark of the

Per-Nils uses grass in his boots to insulate his feet against the cold.

Brit-Marie prepares the birch-bark solution ready for tanning the reindeer hide.

birch tree and then rubs it to create the unique Sami design. Brit-Marie, who was brought up in the traditional Sami way of life, is also a highly skilled tanner, and she showed me the painstaking process involved in taking a rough reindeer hide and transforming it into a soft material used for clothing, boots and knife sheaths. Once the hair has been removed, the hide is soaked in a birch-bark solution in order to soften it before it is scraped over and over again, soaked a second time and then left out to dry. It is then taken inside where it is soaked with hot water and worked until it is soft enough to wear. This is not easy work by any means, but the end product is a fabulously durable, warm and practical piece of material.

I found it uplifting that these old bushcraft skills were still thriving. That had not been the case in many of the ancient communities around the world which I

Brit-Marie demonstrates how she turns tough reindeer hide into a material suitable for clothing.

1. The component parts for making a knife handle: leather, antler and wood 'washers'.

2. The washers slide onto the tang: they must fit properly before gluing.

3. All the components are clamped in place until the glue has hardened.

4. The tang is riveted with the coronet of an antler.

5. The last task is to file and sandpaper the grip until it feels right in your hand.

Yana Mangi, performer of traditional Sami songs

had visited during the year. The erosion of traditional cultures has quickened dramatically in recent years, but the Sami have managed not merely to preserve their heritage for future generations, but to make it work in the modern world.

Perhaps the clearest evidence that Sami culture is alive and well in the modern world is found in the continuing popularity of their traditional songs, known as jojks (pronounced 'yoik'). Traditionally the Sami believe that everything in nature has a soul and they have many gods representing all aspects of the world around them – thunder, wind, reindeer, birds, trees, even stones and rocks. My favourite is the Sami god of wind, who is said to stir up the atmosphere by waving around giant wooden paddles. It may sound quaint or naïve, but if you have ever camped out in the Swedish wilderness and felt and heard the wind swirling around you, you will fully understand the aptness of the image.

It is through the jojk that the Sami express their respect and reverence for nature and while we were there we were lucky enough to meet Yana Mangi, the best-known exponent of the ancient art in Sweden today. Like many Sami people of her generation Yana grew up hearing the jojk and although she now lives in a town and her songs are recorded digitally and listened to on CD players, her heart and soul are rooted in the Swedish forests and it is there that she heads as often as possible for solace and inspiration. The jojk is a spiritual experience both for the singer and for those listening and it was a privilege to sit by a fire in the forest, hearing her sing her homage to the world around us. She told me: 'It is not a question of simply yearning for nature and the forests. It's a question of addiction. The Sami cannot live without it. That'll never go completely because it's in our genes. I live in a modern house but as soon as I go outside I am part of nature.

These pine stumps contain so much resin that they can be lit to provide a good natural stove.

My soul is nature. I am nature.'

A few weeks after we sat in that spot the landscape was transformed by the onset of winter. The entire forest was covered in deep snow and the lakes and rivers had frozen over. The only visible signs of vegetation were the needles and branches of the pine trees.

At one time Sweden's forests were inhabited by bears, wolves, arctic foxes and lynxes, but today there are few wild animals to be found. Unless you know what you are doing and what you are looking for, food can be hard to come by in the Arctic wilderness in the depths of winter, but one excellent source of nutrition are the fish to be found below the frozen surface of lakes. It is one of the great pleasures of camping in these parts to get up on a freezing winter morning, unhook your fish from the ice-hole you have made the day before and cook it over a blazing fire for your breakfast.

In mid-winter the ice will be roughly one metre thick and you could safely drive a car across it, but at other times you have to be more careful. The ice is often at its weakest at the water's edge, but as a general rule of thumb it is safe to walk on if it is more than twenty centimetres thick. When ice fishing, the first step is to clear an area of snow so that you can cut a hole through the ice using an ice chisel or an ice auger, a tool which resembles a large corkscrew. You have to kneel down to make the hole and it is advisable to use a pile of spruce cuttings to insulate you from the cold of the ice. The Sami used sticks as rods and after sinking the line through the hole, they left it overnight and retired to the warmth of their tents to await breakfast.

The early morning is my favourite time of day in the Arctic because more often than not you emerge from your tent to discover that a clean layer of snow has transformed the landscape from the day before. The fresh fall has covered yesterday's tracks, so every day feels like a new beginning.

A journey by dog sledge across the Arctic wilderness is a fantastic experience – and the dog sledge is still an important method of transport when snow mobiles are not available.

By October there is already snow in these northern forests:
within a month this river will be a sheet of solid ice.

Four Seasons

For many years I have travelled to remote corners of the world to observe and practise the skills of bushcraft, but I am never happier than when I step out of my back door and head out to enjoy the beauty and variety of our own countryside, whatever the season. It was, after all, the natural surroundings on my very doorstep that sparked my interest in wildlife and the outdoors in the first place. We are lucky in Britain to have an abundance of wild plants and animals of our own, as well as four very distinct seasons offering fresh opportunities and different challenges throughout the year. What is even better is that each part of the country offers something different, and there is no better way of appreciating the seasons than to head into the outdoors and set up camp in the midst of the wildlife.

In early March, at first glance British woodland can seem cold and uninviting. Very little seems to be happening, but when you look closely you discover that Mother Nature's plans are actually very well advanced. The tiny buds of birch leaves, for instance, are fully formed by now and all they need to burst open is one last surge of energy which they get from the sap beneath the bark. The sap pumps up for just two or three weeks every year and when it starts to work its magic you know that spring has arrived, despite appearances. The birch is a remarkably versatile tree: in the spring you can drink the sap which is packed with goodness, while the bark provides the best tinder for starting fires all year round. The wood is good for carving, which is one of my favourite summer pastimes, and in the autumn the tree provides a home for the birch polypore, a fungus that helps sharpen your knife and also makes good plasters.

Collecting the sap from a birch tree is reasonably straightforward and not at all as damaging as it might appear. To make a natural funnel, or tap, to insert into the tree, look for a branch with a slight kink in it so that you can hang a billy-can over it to collect the sap. Carve a groove along the length of the wood so that the liquid can run down into the container, which you cover with a layer of cloth to stop other bits of the forest falling into it. The sap will start to appear immediately and when you return the following morning you will find a great quantity of sap, which provides a very welcome drink packed with sugar and vitamin C. Modern research has found that birch sap also contains cancer-healing properties. For me, it is the very taste of spring, and I enjoy it most when it is frozen into ice cubes with a mint leaf and then dropped into a single malt whisky. Having enjoyed this gift of nature, I always fulfil my part of our unspoken bargain. Left untouched, the tree could either lose all its sap or get infected through the open cut I have bored with an auger, and the simple way to prevent this is to fashion a plug from a piece of wood and push it into the hole so that it fits snugly.

When living out in the woods I like to sleep under a tarp, which is an incredibly versatile piece of equipment, but where you position your camp could make the difference between a good night's sleep and a nightmare if you are in a woodland with a lot of beech trees, because beech have a tendency to drop huge branches with no warning. It is also advisable to set up camp in an area protected from the wind by thick bush growth and the slope of a hill.

Lighting a fire in the deciduous woods of Britain should never present too many difficulties as there is such an abundance of fuel, kindling and lighting material to hand. Whenever possible, and wherever you are in the world, it is essential to get permission from those who own the land before you start camping or lighting fires. Before lighting the fire, sweep away the leaves to expose the bare earth, and then build and tend it so that only the ends of the logs are left in the morning, because then all you have to clean away is the ash. To get rid of any remaining heat, I always douse the ash with water and then scatter it about the site by hand to make sure nothing is still smouldering. It is important too to feel if the soil is hot because underground roots can catch fire long after you have moved on. Nature provides us with the firewood, and clearing up after you is a small price to pay for the service.

It is a fantastic experience to wake up to the sights, sounds and smells of the woods, but there is nothing worse than a bad night's sleep in the wild, and it is essential to have a waterproof, windproof sleeping bag and an inflatable sleeping mat so that you do not wake up with a cold back. It is an especially enchanting experience in the spring when the forest has come alive after the winter months. Every leaf, every plant, every tree radiates vitality. It is still fairly quiet at this time of year because the migrant birds are yet to return and only native species like the blackbird and robin are singing, but you will find plenty going on if you take more than just a cursory glance at your surroundings.

The bluebells are everywhere, dominating the scene in a dazzling spread of colour, and hiding amongst them are a number of really useful plants, such as the redcurrant whose fruits are developing nicely by this time. In the shade at the base of the redcurrant you might find little wood sorrel leaves, which look a bit like clover, and have a delicious taste like apple peel. Then there is the pignut flower whose nutlike, peppery tubers make for a lovely spring delicacy. In the woodland, the ferns are just starting to unfurl, while the early purple orchid, the hawthorn and the mayflower are all emerging. Out on the heath, the gorse is starting its first flush alongside the crab-apple blossom and the louse-wort.

Ramsons are a very popular wild food because their beautiful white flowers and pungent smell make them easy to identify. The mature leaves are a little too strong for my own culinary taste and I prefer the tender, delicately flavoured baby leaves, perfect for a green salad in the wild. The hardest part of a salad to recreate is the large lettuce leaf component, but perhaps the best

Ramsons: These wild onions carpet the floor of wet woodland throughout the spring and early summer. Their flowers can bring a delicate and delightful flavour to a wild salad.

Birch: in the first few weeks of March the very early stirring of spring brings us an unusual harvest, the sap from the silver birch. By tapping into the bark with a drill and wooden spike or plastic tubing, gallons of this healthful tonic can be collected overnight. Traditionally this fluid was converted to beer or wine. But my preference is to drink it fresh and cold just as it comes from the tree.

solution is to use the young leaves of the lime tree, while the fresh blossom of the crab-apple adds a nice sweet tang. The salad I made was to accompany a simple kebab of tomato and salami, which tastes delicious when cooked. Salami is a really useful provision to carry with you as an emergency food because it has a lot of fat and protein in it that helps to keep you warm.

To skewer the kebab you need a straight stick that is still living, because a dead one would burn and disintegrate. It is best to go for the shoot of a tree that will grow back vigorously such as those of the sweet chestnut. I like to use a saw to trim off the branch because it is neat and surgical and allows the tree to heal quickly and protect itself from bacteria and fungi.

There are a number of ways to build a fire as well as a wide variety of different types of wood in Britain which all burn slightly differently from each other. The type of fire and the type of wood you choose depends on how you plan to use the fire. On some occasions you might want a fire with a lot of flame or one that produces a lot of ash, but when cooking, a fire that produces a great deal of heat is ideal. To cook my kebab I opted for some dead oak branches which burn very hot and very slowly like coal. It is important to strip off the bark from your skewer branch, partly because it is unlikely to be perfectly clean, but also because it can leave a nasty taste on what you are cooking and it is also easier to slide your tomato and salami on.

May is all about new growth – tender leaves, early spring flowers, young shoots – and it is also an incredibly busy month in terms of wildlife as the hibernating animals emerge blinking into the light. It was catching glimpses of these animals that fired my interest in bushcraft as a young boy. Observing the larger mammals of Britain can be very challenging because many of them are nocturnal, but you can gain a fascinating insight into their activities

by piecing together the signs and traces – the tracks – which they leave behind in the night. To track you have to look at your surroundings in an entirely different way. You have to slow down and observe the detail.

The area around where I camped in spring was strewn with badger holes and there were plenty of tell-tale signs to show me which ones were still occupied. At the mouth of one hole there was some badger's hair, which you can identify because it is a little bit springy, rather like our own hair; there was a piece of fresh bracken frond that had been broken off within the previous twelve hours, and a few feet away there was a bluebell bulb that had recently been dug up. Badgers like to eat bluebells and when you walk through the woods at twilight you can often hear their curious munching sound, like a group of picnickers devouring a jar of pickled onions. When searching for insects, badgers like to claw off the bark of trees and fallen branches, leaving behind very distinct scratches on the wood. Recognising animal tracks is a difficult but useful skill to learn and on this occasion I made a track trap by clearing away some leaves close to the sett and creating a patch of sand.

Badgers are incredibly short-sighted and they rely on scent to tell them what is happening around them; so it is important to make sure you know which way the wind is blowing when you set about finding a position from which to observe them as they start to appear after sunset. I chose to sit at the foot of a large beech tree where there was an overhang creating a bit of shadow, and I could be comfortable and still as I leant up against its trunk. It is also a good idea to wrap up warm in dark clothing because you will be barely moving for a long period of time. Patience is a virtue when observing wildlife. 'Sit still, look long, and hold yourself quiet' is the sound advice to deerstalkers somebody once carved into the high seat of a tree in the New Forest. The appearance of a roe deer told me that my own camouflage and choice of observation position were working, and shortly afterwards half a dozen badgers emerged from the darkness and began sniffing the ground in search of their evening meal, as if in a scene from a cartoon. What a privilege it was to sit there watching these extraordinary animals going about their nocturnal lives, oblivious to the humans in their presence. The following morning we returned to inspect the track trap and sure enough the badgers had been very helpful by leaving us perfect footprints.

Badger: unless you are happy to spend time outdoors at night you're unlikely to see badgers in the wild. But if you do you'll discover that these stripe-faced cousins are real clowns of the forest who literally follow their noses. Having shared countless evenings alongside these beautiful animals, I find it impossible to understand how anyone could gain enjoyment from causing them cruelty and suffering.

Red currants: real jewels of our woodland harvest, red currants ripen in the early summer. Today, however, few people are found gathering these wonderful fruits. Perhaps as our lives grow faster and more busy the woodland grows quieter.

July is a wonderful month with its warm sunshine, lush vegetation and the sights and sounds of all the migrant birds back for their annual visit. What I like most about this time of the year is finding a quiet piece of woodland where I can sit down and practise a few skills. The best way to find that quiet piece of woodland is to climb a hill and cast your eyes over the canopy below. When I look at the woods I try to see them through the eyes of our ancestors. They knew all of the trees in the forest with intimacy because they all had a meaning and relevance to their lives. In one small area of British woodland you will often find a whole variety of different trees such as willow, oak, birch, ash, beech and hazel – and if you are wanting to use one of them for a resource it is best to leave the shadows of the forest to find the tree you are looking for.

Another useful tool in the bushman's store of knowledge is understanding how each wood carves and on this occasion I planned to make a breadboard from sweet chestnut, with some string from willow bark to hang it up. Making string is one of the many uses to which willow can be put and for the best results you need to choose shoots which are slightly thicker than your wrist. I have always felt that it is important to make good or replace whatever you take from nature as best you can, and when I chop down a large willow branch I always cut off a number of smaller shoots and plant them in the ground nearby.

Making cord is quite a long process. Take some damp ashes from an old fire and

boil them up in a pot to create a lye solution before adding the strips of bark. Make sure to strip off the outer bark and use the inner because it is stronger and more flexible. For my breadboard I needed a fairly hard wood that would split easily – and the sweet chestnut is the best of them all in this respect. It is a lovely wood, full of tannin, with a lovely smell and very distinctive annual growth rings. It is strong, flexible and rots slowly, making it ideal for the construction of long-term shelters, but it is not good for burning as it spits furiously. The tannin in the wood will also pit your tools too unless you clean them well afterwards.

Once you have split the wood, pare down your chosen piece to a reasonable thickness using a sharp axe. Carving is hard work on the wrists and hands, so it is a good idea to have another job on the go at the same time – such as making the string – so that you can take periodic rests from it. Remove the bark strips after about an hour of simmering and then hang them up to dry. In the meantime you can embellish your board by carving on it some kind of design to give it a bit of character, and you can also make a hole in the handle for the string to go through. The fibres of the cordage need to be a little damp before you start converting it into string. To do so, gently turn both strands in the same direction and they will twist together naturally, before finishing off the length with a reef knot.

There is something especially satisfying about fashioning your own piece of equipment from entirely natural resources – something which you can carry with you for ever in the outdoors in the knowledge that one day it will be returned to the earth from which it sprang.

Pignut: this edible root tastes like a radish – it's a real delight abundant in May–June although, just like our ancestors, the observant forager can sometimes find them in warm places as early as late February.

Blackberries: still our most popular wild fruit, this plant encourages children to grow tall as they reach over the bramble thorns for the biggest juiciest fruits.

In autumn there is nowhere I would rather be than in Scotland. It is simply magnificent. I love it so much, especially in the Highlands, that I have organised a month's work there every autumn since my first visit some twenty years ago. The whole landscape is great for bushcraft but my favourite place to start is up in the hills, in the company of someone who knows them intimately, before setting out to look for the wild red deer. On my most recent visit there I met up with Peter, a stalker on the Rothiemurchus Estate in the heart of the Cairngorm mountains.

Red deer live wild in this delicate landscape and as there are no longer any natural predators, their numbers have to be controlled. Peter manages the herds, searching out the weak and the old for culling, so if anyone knows where to find deer it is him. Being in the right place at the right time is the challenge. The annual rut usually starts in the first week of October and lasts around a month, and if you do manage to catch this magnificent sight it is relatively easy to stalk the deer – so long as the wind is favourable.

In the valleys that nestle between the Highlands there are other challenges for the follower of bushcraft, including acres of ancient forest and an awful lot of water. This region is notorious for its moisture and that can make fire-lighting a challenge. Queen Victoria once had a problem on a picnic in these parts when her trusty manservant, Mr Brown, was unable to get a fire going to brew up a pot of tea. There is, however, a cunning way of lighting a fire in the rain or in sodden conditions. Cut a fallen log into chunks, avoiding the knots as you do so, and even though the wood may have been lying around for a long time, most of it will still be dry on the inside. Splitting it means you can expose the dry bits, and split wood always burns better than whole pieces. To get the fire going, Mr Brown would have had more luck if he had made some feathersticks, by scraping a piece of wood downwards into a collection of thin shavings. If you make tiny slivers alongside the larger shavings, they should be thin enough to catch light from just a single spark and the rest of the feathersticks will then act as kindling.

In these parts it is important to light a fire close to a stream because the peaty ground burns easily. (Peat, in fact, is used on most of the fires in the cottages in this area.) If you light a fire up in the woods around here it can smoulder unnoticed for months before returning to the surface and starting a forest fire. Normally I would not make a fire at all in these surroundings, but if I have to, I head down to the gravel by the river where the ground is not going to catch fire and I can put out the fire easily with water from the river. Furthermore, when the floods come all the ashes left behind will be washed away, leaving no trace.

And so to winter, when the woods are calm and quiet again, and the dial of the seasons has turned full circle. With most of the forest asleep again or resting, it is a bit like wandering into a theatre after the performance – there is a powerful sense of great activity recently come to an end. At this time of year it is great to have a tent with a wood-burning stove, which uses less fuel than a fire and leaves no scar on the ground; and if it is wet outside, it does not matter because you are in a home

from home. Similar to those used by Native Americans, the tipi-style structure was originally designed for use in Arctic countries and I have spent many months living happily at minus 30 degrees centigrade.

Short winter days tend to focus the brain because you barely have time to sort out the essentials like firewood before the sun sets. But with the evenings long and warm, winter does tend to make me reflect on the year that has been. In this particular year, I have been privileged to contemplate all the seasons in Britain from up close while also travelling to many other parts of the world. I have met a host of wonderful people from different pockets of the globe, many of them trying to live their traditional way in the face of ridicule and misunderstanding. It was a joy to share the skills of the Canadians still endeavouring to make canoes in the time-honoured way, but the most memorable visit for me was to Venezuela where the Indians are losing their skills because they are seen by some as outdated and worthless. The highlight of the trip was showing Benito and Saul how to light a fire. This was a traditional skill that had been lost and their joy – and mine – was overwhelming when they achieved it.

I firmly believe that far from damaging the planet, a knowledge of bushcraft can help our natural world. When you see bushcraft skills employed, you may think that we are simply consuming natural resources, but in fact our hands are being very carefully guided by an underlying principle. The more you learn about the trees and the plants the more you respect them. The more you respect them the more you cherish, nurture and look after them. That is the principle of bushcraft.

Red Deer stag: the bellowing of Red Deer stags in the rut is a primeval sound that stirs the soul like no other sound in nature. With the coming of the first frosts these regal beasts compete for harems, oblivious to everything but their deepest carnal desires. These magnificent animals remind us of the potency of nature and the wonder of natural selection.

Scottish Highlands in autumn: truly God's country, I can think of nowhere else on our planet that I would rather be than here in the autumn.

Photography

Photographs for this project were mostly taken as transparencies using both 35mm and 120 stock. Fujichrome Velvia 100F accounts for the majority of images, with some also taken using Fujichrome Provia 100F and Fujichrome 400F.

Camera equipment was largely dictated by the nature of transport in the differing locations. Where portability was not an issue, Nikon 35mm SLR equipment was used.

Where portability placed a premium on lightweight and small size, or where images had to be recorded in very low light, a Leica 35mm rangefinder was employed.

During the filming both the Mamiya 7 and the Leica M7 survived a major helicopter crash - testimony to the excellent build qualities of these cameras.

Panoramic images were recorded using the excellent Hasselblad X-Pan.

Medium format shots were taken at 6 x 7 cm on a Mamiya 7, providing extremely high resolution images for very little equipment weight.

My thanks go to Hardy Hasse from Haselblad UK and Nobby Clarke at Leica Optics for their help and advice.

The Leica M7 was still working after walking away from the crash.
Blurring is caused by aviation fuel that flooded the body.

Acknowledgements

Film

Fujichrome Velvia 100F

Fujichrome Provia 100F

Fujichrome 400F

Camera Equipment

35mm Single Lens Reflex

Nikon F5

Nikon F100

300mm AF-S Nikkor 1:2.8 D

80-200mm AF-S Nikkor 1:2.8 D

17-35mm AF-S Nikkor 1:2.8 D

60mm AF Micro Nikkor 1:2.8D

35mm Rangefinder

Leica M7

35mm Summicron 1:2 ASPH

90mm Apo-Summicron 1:2 ASPH

50mm Noctilux 1:1

24mm Elmarit-M 1:2.8 ASPH

Medium Format

Hasselblad Xpan

45mm 1:4

Mamiya 7

Mamiya 65mmL 1:4

Mamiya 150mmL 1:4.5

This book, and the television series it accompanies would not have been possible without the help of a large number of people throughout the world: to list them all would take up many pages. I would also like to thank Niall Edworthy, who was the guiding light behind the text; Ben Southwell and his team at the BBC; Ned Hoste of 2H who designed the book. And, as always, special thanks to Rachel who kept the home fires burning.

I'm also very grateful to the following for permission to reproduce their photographs: Margaret Charko (Grey Owl), Staffan Hahr (dog-sledging), Barrie Foster, Ben Southwell, Cassie Walkling.

Additional picture sources © Terry Andrewartha/naturepl.com (bluebell wood); © NHPA/Laurie Campbell (badger and red deer).

A DVD of the BBC television programmes which accompany this book – with special features including unseen material filmed for the bushcraft enthusiast – is available through the usual retail outlets or direct from www.raymears.com